PRAEGER WORLD OF ART SERIES

ART OF
THE
Romantic
Era

ART OF THE
Romantic Era

ROMANTICISM · CLASSICISM
REALISM

Marcel Brion

FREDERICK A. PRAEGER, Publishers
NEW YORK · WASHINGTON

BOOKS THAT MATTER

PUBLISHED IN THE UNITED STATES OF AMERICA IN 1966
BY FREDERICK A. PRAEGER, INC., PUBLISHERS
111 FOURTH AVENUE, NEW YORK 3, N.Y.

ALL RIGHTS RESERVED

© COPYRIGHT 1966 BY THAMES AND HUDSON, LONDON
LIBRARY OF CONGRESS CATALOG CARD NUMBER: 65-20070
PRINTED IN GREAT BRITAIN

Contents

Introduction

The transformations which appear in the nineteenth century, first in European art and then in the art of the United States, are partly the consequence of a far-reaching revolution in the realm of aesthetics and partly of crucial changes in thought generally during the period extending from the end of Classicism to the beginning of Romanticism. Of course it is impossible to determine precisely where such periods begin and end, because both thought and feeling for form develop in a manner which will not submit to strict chronological divisions. All the great periods of history and art are interwoven and marked by undercurrents which are almost imperceptible to the observer who sees only what actually happens and not what is beginning to happen. There is no satisfactory way of discriminating, for example, between the three periods of the Baroque—Mannerism, which manifests a transition from the forms and ideas of the Renaissance, Baroque proper (especially in its dramatic leanings), and Rococo, which is not an 'ageing Baroque' but a different orientation in a new Baroque style just as authentic as its predecessor. Likewise, certain artists who genuinely belong to the Rococo period of the Baroque—Watteau, Maulbertsch, Tiepolo—can be considered not only as precursors of Romanticism, but as painters in whose work we recognize certain Romantic elements which, in their turn, influence not only later painters but also—and even more strongly—certain habits of thinking and feeling which are peculiarly Romantic.

In this interpretation of succeeding aesthetic trends, one must distinguish between different ways of thinking and feeling and between the various methods of expression. Complex technical problems are involved which there is not space to analyse here. And it is essential for us not to attach too much importance to those seemingly valuable categories which would mark the boundary between this and that movement. For example, it is evident that if one considers the Realism of the middle of the nineteenth century as a reaction to the Romanticism which was then in decline, one observes in Romanticism a desire, which is both obvious and very precisely defined (especially in Germany and France), to reanimate a concept of the Real which had been weakened if not rejected altogether by the thought of Rococo and Classical artists. In Delacroix's *Liberty Leading the People* (*Ill. 138*) and Géricault's *Raft of the 'Medusa'* (*Ill. 142*) the desire for absolute realism in execution dominates the Romantic sentiment which inspires such subjects.

But the heritage of the past remains within all the great aesthetic transformations, allied to a presentiment of the future and to a desire to translate into artistic terms a characteristic moment in the development of man. And yet one also finds that in the same artist diverse and often contradictory forces may co-exist. The work of Gustave Courbet (*Ill. 151*) is a good example of this. Courbet wished to be rigidly realistic and indeed claimed to have based an entire doctrine and system on Realism, but nonetheless certain Romantic elements do survive in his paintings. Similarly, traces of Romanticism are found in the paintings of François Millet (*Ills. 153, 154*), who was a Realist by intention but a Romantic by temperament. The work of both men will hardly fit a definition which claims to retain only certain specific characteristics at the expense of those instinctive features which must always be taken into account.

If it is evident that Romanticism already existed, whether active or dormant, in certain artists of the eighteenth century (and it would be ridiculous to refuse to recognize it), it is equally evident that it was deeply rooted in the Baroque, especially with regard to German painting, where it appeared with an instinctive organic and biological flair which openly opposed itself to all that was arbitrary and artificial in Classicism. Classicism in Germany—even more than in France, where the rational spirit of Classicism dominated even its vagaries and errors—renounced the vitality and vivifying force of instinct and immured itself in concepts and forms inherited from antiquity. But one must not forget that the great 'systematizers' of Classicism— whether David or Winckelmann, whose thinking obliged art to retreat rather than advance, or Wedgwood's *Etruria*—harked back to an antiquity which they knew only through Roman copies of lost Greek originals, or through the discoveries made in the villas of Campagna that had been entombed in the ashes and lava of Vesuvius, where there was preserved a civilization already in decline.

This arbitrary, artificial aspect of Classicism, rationalistic rather than instinctive, which contented itself with imitations of imitations of a still unknown Greek art, provoked the reaction called Romanticism, whose ambition was to recapture and express all that the Classicists had banished. But in analysing the aesthetic changes which appear at any given time, we must remember the historical, political, social and even economic factors which are closely related to them. The popular side of Romanticism is obviously a legacy of the French Revolution and of the Napoleonic empire which the revolution spawned—in opposition to all which made, or seemed to make, the Rococo an art of the court. Similarly, the advent, around the middle of the nineteenth century, of Realism, which aimed at completing the return to reality already manifest in Romanticism, was sustained by a set of social and political concepts. These ideas, which managed to become preponderant during this period, were themselves the causes or effects of doctrines such as the almost superstitious belief in Progress, the positivism reigning despotically in philosophical thinking, and the intrusion into the domain of art of a belief in a System, evidence of which we find in Courbet when he says: 'I believe that painting is an essentially concrete art which can only consist of the representation of things which are real and which exist.' The veneration of the Achievement in the realm of history, philosophy or science contaminates art in proportion to its interference with the phenomena of aesthetic expression.

Therefore it is significant that to a century which is so faithfully mirrored in its art, new values and a new direction were given by the repercussions of all those changes in society brought about by the glorification of the proletariat and their work, the progress of industry and the revelation of the new-born beauty of the machine, and the imperatives which appeared in the work of the theoreticians of socialism, Proudhon and Karl Marx, or, on the purely literary

9

plane, in Balzac, Dickens and George Sand. Events themselves influenced artistic creation: Robert Schumann, however far removed he may have been from political preoccupations, composed, during the feverish days of the revolt in Dresden in 1848, his four marches for piano, *Opus 76*, entitled *Barricades*; and Richard Wagner, who certainly had nothing of the socialist leader about him, led (with Michael Bakunin) an insurrection in the Saxon capital.

These social, political and economic happenings gave the trend to Realism a kind of popular vindication as a consequence of a new awareness of the existence of an industrial proletariat, itself a novel phenomenon of the second half of the nineteenth century—a time disturbed by the fever of industrialization. The worker is the hero of Naturalistic novels, those of Emile Zola for instance, as the gentleman was the hero of eighteenth-century literature and the bourgeois the typical character of the Biedermeier era. The peasant, no longer idyllic or pastoral, is primitive, almost bestial, with the same nature and even the same colouring as the land he tills. Together they incarnate the human struggle, the human misery which the Realists wanted to depict with Naturalistic exactitude.

If it were possible to distinguish one absolute difference between Realism and Naturalism, it would lie in the extent to which Realism approaches observation and portrayal of the day-to-day essence of things and beings, while adding to this objective truth as much as it can contain of the subjective feelings of the artist. Naturalism, on the other hand, claimed objectivity pure and simple—in a sense, no more than a photographic record of objective truth. To see this difference at work, compare a Bastien-Lepage (*Ill. 162*) or an Uhde with one of those pictures by Courbet or Millet in which the feeling or inherent emotion which had dictated the treatment has more importance than the subject itself.

This cult of the Achievement, a new and soon predominant element in the philosophical thinking of the latter half of the nineteenth century, corresponds to the artist's need for objectivity— an objectivity which signifies a rejection of the intimate participation which had been one of the most generous and stirring factors in Romanticism. The Naturalist believed, even more strictly than the

Realist, in the Achievement, in the actual event and in the thing itself for its own sake. This naturally entails an impoverishment in the spiritual content of the work of art, whose purpose for the Naturalist seems to be to equal the impersonality of the snapshot, and undoubtedly the invention and rapid development of photography gave birth to a new way of looking at things, of experiencing what one sees and, in the case of the artist, of depicting them. The simultaneous appearance of the inhuman eye of the camera and of this wish to withhold personal feeling from painting, leaving nothing but the meticulous precision of sheer materiality, is too striking for us to resist the conclusion that here art was influenced by the creations of industry, both in its concepts and its way of expressing them.

The example of Courbet, Millet and Hans Thoma, and even more perhaps of the Italian Verists who wanted to purge Realism of every vestige of Romanticism, shows that the transition from one artistic movement to another is more subtle and often more hypothetical than one would suppose. A firm resolve to 'return to the Real' had been the driving force of the Romantics after the artifices of the Rococo and Classical periods, and their depiction—albeit more subjective than objective—of this reality was enough to unleash against them the anger of critics faithful to academic traditions. Similarly, the persistence of Romantic emotion in what artists such as Thoma (*Ills. 110, 111*) or Favretto believed to be everyday reality prevented the erection at some given moment in the nineteenth century of a clearly recognizable and indisputable frontier dividing the moments when Romanticism ended and Realism began.

The distinction between Realism and Naturalism, notwithstanding what has already been said, is equally uncertain. However, no equivocation is possible with reference to the actual substance of Romanticism. It is a phenomenon of aesthetics both so general and so particular (and so particularized in different countries) that we should confine our attention to its definition and, more specifically, to its diverse expressions and essential qualities.

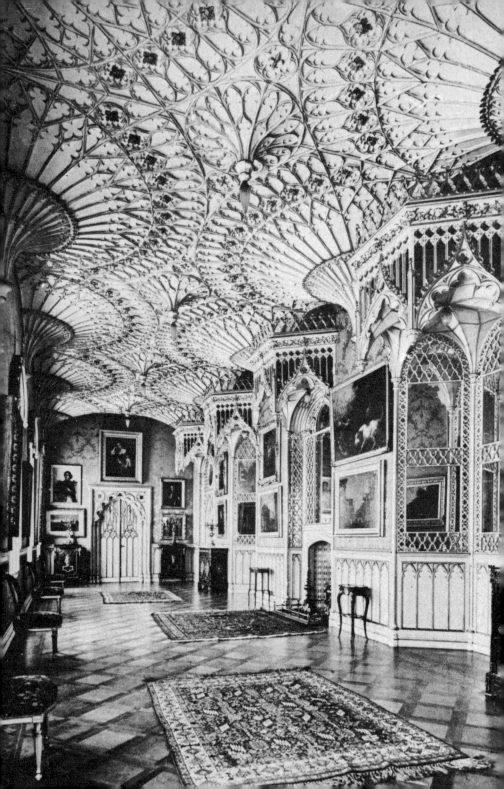

CHAPTER ONE

Architecture

The aesthetic phenomenon we call Romanticism is not easily placed in a particular period or a particular place, for it is a condition of the human consciousness which manifests itself, often simultaneously, in the infinitely varied domains of art, philosophy, music and poetry. Indeed its reflections can be seen even in the realms of science and sociology. But when one tries to define Romanticism by opposing it to Classicism, which should be its opposite, one ends up only with artificial, arbitrary and negative conclusions. Yet, on the other hand, when it is examined alone we find it just as difficult to make anything out of this mixture of forms and ideas which we are accustomed to call Romantic. From all sides and in all directions are fused those unique features of unrest, of a notion of Becoming, of feelings— feeling for nature, for the infinite and for distant pastures, for solitude, for the tragedy of Being and the inaccessible ideal—which constitute the principal elements of Romantic art.

Artistic forms speak more eloquently than definitions. Schumann's symphonies, Caspar David Friedrich's landscapes and *Childe Harold's Pilgrimage* all bear witness to the nature and essence of Romanticism more forcefully than any erudite commentary. One cannot reach the substance of Romanticism by dialectical routes: only an immediate and total communion reveals that deep reality which reason alone will never uncover. Likewise, one can automatically consider as false any claim to determine with absolute certainty whether one artist is Romantic or another is not. Chronological classifications are of no help in a field whose dimensions are not so clearly marked as the historians sometimes wish. At what time did Romanticism begin, at what time did it end? Such questions cannot be answered without inviting the reader to examine first his own sensibility, and to decide which painting or music arouses in him the excitement,

◄ I   HORACE WALPOLE (1717–97)   *The Gothic Gallery, Strawberry Hill*

the nostalgia and the anxieties indissolubly linked with Romanticism.

One risks losing sight of the essential phenomenon by extending too far one's field of vision: it is wiser, I think, to reduce the area under observation in order to study more precisely the artistic expression which it accommodates. For this reason I propose to deal mainly with the century from 1750 to 1850, not to satisfy any predetermined chronology, but because during this period Romanticism shone most brightly and produced the most splendid flowering of forms and ideas which it ever achieved. Of course it would be interesting to follow and trace the undercurrents as well as the main stream, and thus to discover factors which anticipate or prolong the movement, but the scope of this book does not permit such explorations.

It is by contact and communion with the works themselves that an exact idea may be articulated of what is authentically Romantic in them, especially if one receives them with the heart at least as much as with the intelligence. In fact this was one of the ambitions of the Romantics, to create a *total work of art*, that is to say one which addresses itself simultaneously to all the senses, to the sensibility, to the emotions, and to the intelligence. This vague concept of the 'work of art of the future' communicates from different premises, but in the same spirit, in the works of Philipp Otto Runge (*Ills. 107–9*) and Richard Wagner, proclaiming the universality of its perceptions; it wants to be accepted simultaneously in music, poetry and the plastic arts. In this desperate pursuit of totality we may clearly perceive one of the principal sources of the Romantic spirit: the supposition that an emotion is not complete if all the senses do not work together to arouse it.

Although the artist could not realize this fantastic ambition of an impossible totality, his work demanded that it should be contemplated at once as music, as poetry and as a plastic form, although it might not be more in itself than a symphony, a poem or a picture. The point is that one should *listen* to a Romantic painting in order to reach the music it contains, and this is one of the keys to a deeper understanding of that secret quality which remains hidden if one looks at a Romantic painting as one would look at any other.

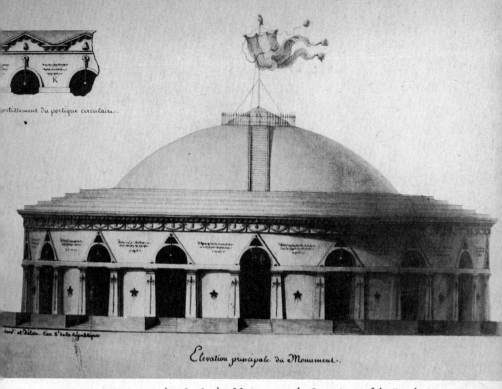

Elevation principale du Monument.

2 JEAN JACQUES LEQUEU (1758–1825) *Monument to the Sovereignty of the People*

The portrayable never became a goal for the Romantics because the communicable seeks out those zones of the spectator's consciousness which are moved not only by the visual and the tangible, but which are also set in motion by strong human sentiment. Because it depicts man in his nostalgia, in his unrest and in that confused mixture of aspirations and melancholy called *Sehnsucht*, and because it would awaken in the hearts of those who see it the same sentiments as those from which it derives, becoming in its subject at once poetry and music as much as painting, the Romantic picture demands of us nothing less than complete involvement.

Reluctant as I am to predict a 'return to Romanticism' by the artists of today, one cannot afford to remain insensible to the appeal

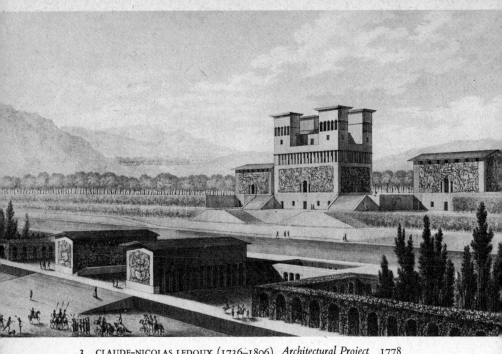

3   CLAUDE–NICOLAS LEDOUX (1736–1806) *Architectural Project*   1778

4   CLAUDE–NICOLAS LEDOUX *House of the Surveyor of the Loue*

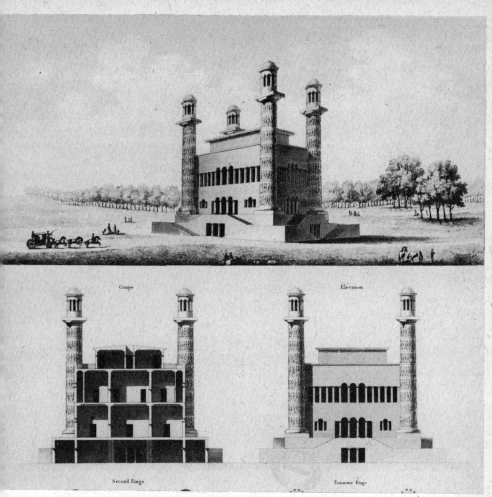

5   CLAUDE-NICOLAS LEDOUX   *Memorial in Honour of Womankind*

which this art has for us, however distant from it we may consider ourselves. Its vitality is not certified by the art historians alone, any more than they are led to do it justice solely under the influence of contemporary artistic trends. Rather, its vitality stems from that sympathetic intimacy, both discreetly sonorous and uninsistently emotional, which aims at a whole-hearted communion. The art of the Romantics is a *living* art to which the deep sources of our feelings

17

6 ETIENNE-LOUIS BOULLÉE (1728–99) *Entrance to a Cemetery*

respond. It owes nothing to fashion, it is eternally valuable and inexhaustibly inspiring precisely because it expresses itself with a warmth of feeling which has never been at odds with the inspiration of any artist, at least when he was capable of testing it.

There was nothing new about the neo-Classic architecture of the end of the eighteenth century. It was content to reproduce the old Greek and Roman 'order' and sometimes to exaggerate the passion for antiquity into fanaticism as, for example, in Wedgwood's *Etruria*. Similarly, Romantic architecture, which was incapable of new invention, also returned to the past and fervently adopted the styles of the Middle Ages, especially the Gothic. The attempts of Ledoux (*Ills. 3–5*), Lequeu (*Ill. 2*) and Boullée (*Ill. 6*) to create an original style, completely different from that which had previously existed, were failures; although such beautiful and surprising constructions as the salt works at Chaux, the ideal city conceived and built by Ledoux, remain an exception. The thinking of these

revolutionaries was too daring and too absolute to have either disciples or successors. But in their dissatisfaction with the Baroque tradition they were pioneers and creators of new forms largely based on elementary geometrical shapes.

The neo-Gothic fathered innumerable imitators; it rarely led to individual creation, except when the ill-interpreted forms and spirit of the past gave birth to the unexpected. The scrupulously exact reproduction of medieval architecture by Pugin and Viollet-le-Duc was in direct contrast to the fantasy which gave a new accent, both piquant and unique, to those works which did not docilely follow the models of the past. We may possibly see the dawning of a new style in such 'follies' as Walpole's Strawberry Hill (*Ills. 1, 11*), but certainly not in the reconstructions by Joseph Daniel Ohlmüller, Sir Charles Barry or Viollet-le-Duc. Archaeological fidelity and respect for the past drained neo-Gothic architecture of all the sap which could have nourished a genuinely novel style.

7 JAMES WYATT (1747–1813) *Fonthill Abbey* 1795–1807

8 JAMES WYATT AND SIR JEFFREY WYATTVILLE (1766–1840) *Ashridge* 1806–17

9 WILLIAM CHAMBERS
(1723–96)
Chinese Pagoda,
Kew Gardens

In assimilating all the styles of the Middle Ages, architects in
Germany attempted to re-create the medieval intellectual life as
much as to give them a new lease of life in eclectic amalgamations
of the forms and conventions of the Byzantine, Romanesque, Gothic
and Renaissance architectures. Wackenroder and later the Boisserée
brothers had imparted the ideal of the Middle Ages to the youth of

21

10 WILLIAM PORDEN (c. 1755–1822) AND JOHN NASH (1752–1835) *Brighton Pavilion* 1803–18

their time, and the jubilee celebrations in honour of Dürer in 1828 had brilliantly confirmed the triumphant resurrection of the Gothic. But in spite of the efforts of architects to revive and reanimate their borrowings from the past, the contributions to Romantic art of Georg Moller, von Heideloff, Schwecten, Ziebland and Rössner produced a rather frigid artificiality, sometimes grandiose but lacking in any truly original inspiration.

In England the Gothic had been so well assimilated into the landscape, ideas and feelings that it was considered the only suitable style for churches or 'temples of learning'—the schools and universities. As a result, a scholastic and ecclesiastical sort of Gothic survived during the seventeenth and eighteenth centuries.

11 HORACE WALPOLE AND WILLIAM ROBINSON (*c.* 1720–75) *Strawberry Hill* 1749–54

The English conviction that Gothic was the only true religious style of architecture predetermined the work of Sir Jeffrey Wyattville (1766–1840) who completed Ashridge in 1817 (*Ill. 8*), Auguste Pugin and his son Augustus Welby Northmore Pugin (1812–52, *Ill. 13*). Through his love of the medieval Augustus was converted to Catholicism and constructed at his own expense the Church of St Augustine at Ramsgate. A student of symbolism, he published in 1833 his *Apology for Christian Architecture* which became gospel for disciples and emulators like Sir George Gilbert Scott (1811–78), who was nicknamed the 'greatest Goth in Europe' (*Ill. 14*), and Sir Charles Barry, who erected Highclere Castle (*Ill. 12*) in the purest Perpendicular.

12   SIR CHARLES BARRY
(1796–1863)
*Highclere Castle,
Hampshire*
1842–*c.* 1855

13   AUGUSTUS WELBY
NORTHMORE PUGIN
(1812–52)
*St Giles Church, Cheadle
(Staffordshire)* 1841–46

14 SIR GEORGE GILBERT SCOTT
(1811–78)
Nikolaikirche, Hamburg
1845–63

The fantastic eclecticism of a man like Kent, who was as much at home in the neo-Gothic as in the neo-Classic, seemed frivolous to the fervent medievalists. Classical or Romantic: the distinction became a kind of religious conviction for Pusey and the Ecclesiological Society, and even a boundary between the generations (it was commonly said that 'men over sixty remain faithful to Palladio; men under sixty have declared for Gothic').

In France, where Classicism was as *innate* as the Gothic, the return to the Middle Ages had the significance of a sentimental and political movement (the Middle Ages stands for the monarchy). But it was also born of an archaeological sympathy founded on a just appreciation of the aesthetic, technical and functional aspects of Gothic. It happened that the architects who 'built medieval' were those who previously had restored churches damaged by the weather or by revolution. The restorations by Debret at Saint-Denis, by Alavoine at

15   F.-C. GAU (1790–1853)   *Church of Sainte Clothilde, Paris*   1846

16   E. H. GODDE (1781–1869) AND J.-B. LESUEUR (1794–1883)   *Hôtel de Ville, Paris*

Rouen and by Duban in the Sainte-Chapelle prepared the way for the construction of the Church of Sainte Clothilde (*Ill. 15*) by Gau in 1846, the Paris Hôtel de Ville (*Ill. 16*) by Godde and Lesueur, the Bibliothèque de Sainte Geneviève (*Ill. 18*) by Labrouste (1801–75) and the Château de Pierrefonds (*Ill. 17*) by Viollet-le-Duc. Creation and copy confound one another, and the copyist makes a virtue of his renunciation. But the new metallic construction, when effectively used, gave an unforeseen sense of soaring grandeur to the Gothic. Still, at times restoration and original creation were confused, as in the work of Viollet-le-Duc, whose good intentions mixed the piety of authentic restoration with the fantasy of personal interpretation, leading him sometimes to be 'more Gothic than the Goths' in his idealization and mythologization of the medieval.

27

17 EUGÈNE EMMANUEL VIOLLET-LE-DUC (1814–79) *Château de Pierrefonds*

Among the architects who first introduced neo-Gothic into the
United States, pride of place must go to Benjamin Latrobe and
Maximilien Godefroy. Not only did they introduce it, they suc-
ceeded in acclimatizing it despite the instinctive hostility of the
country's Protestants to 'majestic monuments of superstition', to
borrow Gibbon's words (this was well before the 'great fury of
1830', as significant in America as in France).

Latrobe (1769–1820) was of English origin and came to Virginia
in 1796 not as an architect but as an engineer. His originality lay
primarily in his ability to adapt ancient styles to the practical and
cultural needs of America. The corncob and tobacco furnished him
with previously unknown decorative motifs, and when the Director
of the Bank of Pennsylvania insisted that he should build them a
pastiche of a Greek temple, Latrobe regretfully resigned. Although

28

he was always proclaiming his attachment to the Attic style as being that most suitable for a democracy, he was familiar with the great buildings of the Middle Ages and they won both his interest and his sympathy. His eclecticism is nowhere better illustrated than in his entries for the 1805 competition for the design of Baltimore Cathedral, when he submitted two designs—one strictly Classical, the other frankly and audaciously neo-Gothic.

The French emigré Maximilien Godefroy (1789–1833) was seventeen years younger than Latrobe and became a professor of architecture in Baltimore. He was more 'Gothic' than Latrobe and combated his predecessor's eclecticism. Ishiel Town (1794–1844) was an even more complex figure than Latrobe or Godefroy.

18 HENRI LABROUSTE (1801–75) *Bibliothèque de Sainte Geneviève, Paris* 1843–50

19 ALEXANDER DAVIS (1803–92) *Blithewood, Robert Donaldson Estate, Fishkill, N.Y.* 1834

Trinity Church in New Haven, Connecticut, springing from what he called 'carpenter's Gothic', signalled his desire no longer to worship exclusively either the neo-Greek or the neo-Roman, of which he had been an enthusiastic partisan. Its Gothic spire and fake vaults demonstrate Town's medievalism, and his association with Alexander Davis (1803–92) marked the flowering of his 'Middle Ages period'. The Yale Library (1840) and New York University (1837) are the result of a considered intention to reproduce in America the ancient Oxford colleges, and Blithewood (*Ill. 19*) is a somewhat earlier attempt to place a 'Gothic' house with gables and a tower in a typically 'Picturesque' garden.

After its triumphs with churches and universities, artificial medievalism won for itself more utilitarian buildings. But 'educa-

20 JAMES RENWICK (1818–95) *Grace Church, New York*

tional Gothic' stayed alive with the 'Anglo-Norman fortress' created by Robert Dale Owen, Robert Mills and James Renwick in 1852 for the Smithsonian Institute; the Wadsworth Atheneum at Hartford flanked by square towers and lit by Tudor windows, which was built by Town, Davis and their pupil Austin; the translation of Westminster Abbey to Yale in 1840 by Town and Davis; and Renwick's Grace Church (*Ill. 20*). The Boston Railway Station of 1847 also resembled an ancient stronghold, complete with keep and watchtower.

*   *   *

In Europe after the middle of the nineteenth century an architectural revolution took place under the influence of those social and economic factors mentioned in the Introduction, and conditioned rather

31

by the invention of new materials, iron and reinforced concrete, than by changes of a purely artistic nature. Yet, so powerful was the rule of the academic tradition of antique and Gothic 'order', there were few spirits at that time capable of being moved by the strange beauty of large metal structures. A conflict began to appear between what we may call the *architecture for artists*, incapable of innovation while believing itself novel in constructing hybrid edifices in which the different styles of the Middle Ages and the Renaissance were associated in unimaginative combinations, and an *architecture for engineers* which was striving for utility and practicality rather than art, and which employed the new products of industry. The laws of supply and demand held sway in the domain of structural engineering; whereas before one thought of architecture only in connection with churches, palaces, town halls and markets, the new orientation of society, with the introduction of the factory and these new inventions, demanded constructions adapted to their needs without forfeiting beauty.

The fashion in all countries in the latter half of the nineteenth century, of holding Universal Exhibitions, harboured a style which was the consequence of the unforeseen possibilities of structural engineering for covering vast areas. This extension of the use of metal was first put into practice where the combination of glass and metal could be most judiciously employed, and from 1833 Rohat de Fleury showed the possibilities of the new technique in the glass halls of Paris.

The movement from mere technique to art in metal architecture led to the ultimate triumph of 'functionalism'. The coincidence of utility and beauty, which aestheticians (especially Alberti) had preached since the beginning of the Renaissance, took on a new significance with the arrival of the industrial era. Undoubtedly the public eye and taste were not sufficiently prepared to recognize the unaccustomed beauties whose advent had not been anticipated by contemporary culture. The taste for the strange and the original led to the theory of 'art for art's sake' which was pushed to extremes (and to absurd extremes by certain groups) in the second half of the century. It was the belief in an 'unpaid-for beauty', coupled with

21 GUSTAVE EIFFEL (1832–1923) *Eiffel Tower, Paris* 1887–89

hostility to any marriage of the useful and the beautiful, that inspired those whom we call the aesthetes (not to be confused with aestheticians!). However, the great success of the popular and exotic arts in the twentieth century shows that a new generation was capable of making that exact correlation between the useful and the beautiful which their predecessors denied was possible.

Architecture in metal was first appreciated for its practical advantages in utilitarian application; it was much later before its beauty was recognized. The violent controversy stirred up by the construction of the Eiffel Tower in Paris, which was probably the first non-utilitarian metal structure, shows how far public opinion still was from unanimity on the merits of an aesthetic derived directly from technology and modelled on it.

22, 23 JOSEPH PAXTON (1803–65) *Crystal Palace after its removal to Sydenham in 1852* (above), and *the interior before installation of exhibits, London,* 1851 (right)

Coignet's use of reinforced concrete after 1852—that is, contemporary with the flowering in Europe of metal construction—seemed to resuscitate an aesthetic comparable to that symbolized in some respects by the Eiffel Tower (*Ill. 21*). But this method failed to develop from an 'architecture for engineers' to an 'architecture for artists', while the Eiffel Tower is a masterpiece on both counts.

One of the principal merits of structural engineering is, as I have said, the possibility of roofing vast areas with the minimum of supports; whence arises that tendency to the gigantic which is found above all in exhibition halls, and which has its apotheosis in the conception and construction of the skyscraper in the United States.

The point at the middle of the nineteenth century which marks the decline of Romanticism and heralds the arrival of Realism also marks the first triumphs of steel: in Paxton's Crystal Palace (*Ills. 22, 23*), in England in 1851, in the Halles of Paris, designed by Baltard in 1853, and in the Sun Building in Baltimore by J. R. G. Hatsfield. The way was now open by which builders would travel in future, despite the stolid resistance put up by the traditionalists. But the expressed concern of the traditionalists did prove to be valuable in reminding younger architects, among whom utility was often the sole consideration, that the ideal of beauty had always been an essential condition for their predecessors.

CHAPTER TWO

Sculpture

Art historians are generally unfair to Romantic sculpture, and too often seem to be limited to the categorical judgments laid down by two eminent representatives of Romanticism. Théophile Gautier stated that 'of all the arts, that which lends itself least to Romantic expression is surely sculpture. She seems to have derived her definitive forms from antiquity. Every sculptor must necessarily be Classical; he is always, at the bottom of his heart, a worshipper of Olympus.' Madame de Staël also perceived a fundamental and irreconcilable contradiction between sculpture, which she deemed a pagan art, and painting, which to her was the Christian art form *par excellence*.

Sculptors gained a new impetus from neo-Classicism, especially in France and England. Funerary art, however, as in the monument to Lord Nelson by John Flaxman (1755–1826) in St Paul's Cathedral, London, and the tomb of Sir Eyre Coote at Westminster by Thomas Banks (1735–1805), attests to the birth of a new spirit in opposition to the dryness of Canova's brand of neo-Classicism.

More originality is to be found in the work of German sculptors such as Gottfried Schadow (1764–1850, *Ill. 24*), Christian Rauch (1777–1857) and Ernst Rietschel (1804–61); but their Romanticism is not nearly equal to that of the painters. In France, on the other hand, perhaps because this country has always been a chosen ground for plastic and three-dimensional expression of sentiment, an original and vigorously accented Romantic statuary began to appear. The French sculptors were greatly influenced by poetry and painting—to such an extent that their feeling was contaminated by a certain pictorialism and one finds them deliberately distancing themselves from the purely plastic.

24 JOHANN GOTTFRIED SCHADOW (1764–1850)
The Princesses Luise and Frederika of Prussia 1795–97

But even in these efforts by Romantic sculptors to obtain effects apparently reserved for painters, one sees a desire to open up and enlarge the field of sculpture. The fantastic bas-reliefs by Antonin Moine (1769–1849) are as 'unsculptural' as possible; in their subjects they recall the engravings of Louis Boulanger, Devéria or Gustave

Doré: *Goblins Abroad* (1831), *Goblins Fighting* (1835) and *Witches'*
Sabbath (1833) were the subjects preferred by an artist who felt
himself so completely cut off from his age that he killed himself to
escape it entirely. Félicie de Fauveau (1799–1886), on the other hand,
enjoyed a long life and lasting success (*Ill. 25*), despite the extrava-
gances of such compositions as the *Monument to Dante* which
brought her fame in 1836. This was a work loaded with pillars, rose
windows, pinnacles, gargoyles, arrows, and symbolic and allegorical
ornaments whose description would fill a book, although the
Monument itself is scarcely six and a half feet high.

The lovable Jehan Duseigneur (1808–66) brought to his work as
to his attire (he cherished velvet doublets) a bizarre mixture of
serious Romanticism and a taste for the 'troubadour'. 'Troubadour'
was a bastard version of the Gothic, the reduction of the monumental to the minuscule, of the dignified to the affected, of feeling to
sentimentality, of sensitivity to silliness. Duseigneur unhappily had

25 FÉLICIE DE FAUVEAU (1799–1886)
Queen Christine of Sweden Refusing to Spare her Equerry Monaldeschi

26 JEHAN DUSEIGNEUR (1808–66) *Orlando Furioso* 1831

more ambition than talent, more dreams than means to realize them. *Orlando Furioso*, 1831 (*Ill. 26*) is his most authentic and vigorous creation.

Auguste Préault (1810–79) is much more interesting, because his work remained untouched by all that was deliberate and artificial in Romantic sculpture (*Ill. 28*). A man of sombre temperament and violent character, he wanted his work to express his social ideas, which inclined to the revolutionary. François Rude (1784–1855), as powerful as Préault but less evanescent, was the man of the *Marseillaise*. His lyricism is at once Napoleonic and social, robust and simple; always ill at ease with the imaginary, he preferred to deal in the visible and tangible. And there is an air of clumsiness and inappropriateness about his *The Imperial Eagle Watching over Napoleon* (*Ill. 27*).

27 FRANÇOIS RUDE (1784–1855)   *The Imperial Eagle Watching over Napoleon*   1845

28 ANTOINE AUGUSTE PRÉAULT (1810–79)   *Massacre*   1834

Since Classical Rome, satiric irony had almost never employed the service of sculpture. It was Romanticism, through the offices of Jean-Pierre Dantan (1800–69) and Honoré Daumier (1808–79), which was the first to use the statuette as a political weapon: Daumier's Realism exaggerated the features of his model to the point of caricature. In portrait sculpture, a passion for reality inspired David d'Angers (1788–1856), who portrayed numerous celebrated contemporaries. But his emotion outweighed his projected simple exactitude; one sees in his work what might be called a lyric realism, which retains much Romanticism rather like those portraits of animals for which Antoine Louis Barye (1796–1875) became famous. Barye worked with living models in museums and in the Zoological Gardens, but there is plenty of Romanticism in his tragic combats between a jaguar and a crocodile (*Ill. 29*) or an elephant and a tiger (*Ill. 30*). As a result of these flights of the imagination he was condemned by David, the systematic theoretician of Classicism, who reproached him because his animals 'were not philosophically conceived'.

29 ANTOINE LOUIS BARYE (1796–1875) *Jaguar Devouring a Crocodile*

30   ANTOINE LOUIS BARYE   *Indian Mounted on an Elephant Killing a Tiger*

The desire to reproduce truth, to keep to the facts and to look for subjects in the workaday world, produces a unique configuration in the work of the greatest of the Naturalist sculptors, Constantin Meunier (1831–1905). In his statues and bas-reliefs as much as in his pictures—for Meunier was also a painter—he glorified the figure of the worker: the blacksmith, the farm labourer, the stevedore. Yet even more important than this feeling for the hard facts of life was

31 JEAN BAPTISTE CARPEAUX
(1827–75)
Dancer with Tambourine

pity and sympathy for human suffering and social inequality. This sympathy made the Belgian sculptor, as it made François Millet, a sort of apostle of new ideas exalting the nobility and dignity of work. In this he was very different from Jean Baptiste Carpeaux (1827–75), who was completely Romantic in his paintings, transfiguring reality in famous compositions like *The Dance* (now in the Paris Opera House). This transfiguration was accompanied by a certain softening that made reality in his portraits at once more elegant and more lovable, and thus Carpeaux (*Ill. 31*) became the chronicler of the light

32 JULES DALOU
(1838–1902)
A Woman Reading
c. 1875

and frivolous beauty which flourished in the Paris of the Second Empire.

Jules Dalou (1838–1902) is a different case altogether (*Ill. 32*). Without going so far as to personify in his figures the effort and dignity of work, as did Meunier, he nonetheless incarnated the socialist ideology to which Realism and Naturalism are closely allied. Exiled in England because of his political opinions, Dalou spent more than twenty years completing his great monument to the *Triumph of the Republic* in Paris, which is at once a powerful piece of

45

sculpture, a genuine profession of faith and a concretization of the ideas that inspired him.

*   *   *

In the foregoing I have taken a rather comprehensive view of some of the many aspects of sculpture and architecture inspired by the various currents of Romanticism and Realism. (The sculptor Auguste Rodin, because of the complexity of his work and his genius, escapes these classifications.) Now we must turn to the painting, which was certainly the most important art during this period and that in which the period's aspirations, ambitions and even the most delicate shadings of its sensibility were deployed. But to examine it properly we will need to abandon our panoramic viewpoint so that we may study the way in which new tendencies in painting were born and how they flourished in those countries where they were most brilliantly affirmed—and, finally, that we may distinguish the numerous pictorial romanticisms and realisms which illustrated the aesthetic evolution of Europe and the United States in the nineteenth century.

CHAPTER THREE

Painting

ENGLAND

One of the sources of English Romantic painting was a considerable change in the character of the feeling for nature—repudiating artificiality and seeking only poetry and truth. Although artists were still going to Italy, in obedience to the convention of the Grand Tour as well as to initiate themselves into Classical beauty, many of them were also freeing themselves from its obligations. For all of them the English landscape became the principal theme of their inspiration, an inexhaustible source of artistic interest and joy, a pure delight for the heart and the senses. And English Romanticism was fed by that inclination towards the supernatural, the irrational, fantasy and the fantastic which is a constant in the British character, and also by being steeped in a poetry in which Milton, Shakespeare and the Bible held pride of place.

One must add to these, after that happy swindle by the master of the Scottish school, MacPherson's *Ossian*, and the scholarly Percy's *Reliques*, two elements of equal importance: first, the authentic, immediate, sincere and spontaneous experiencing of nature; and second, the transposition, frequently unconscious, of verbal poetry into pictorial poetry. These elements conjoined to form the personality of the first Romantics, in particular William Blake, John Martin and John Flaxman (although Flaxman had an ambition to be Classical—Dante and Aeschylus inspired his compositions, which vibrate with a kind of graphic Romanticism—*Ill. 35*—comparable to that of Carstens). To these we should add the influence of Fuseli (pp. 191–3); both by his example and his teaching this Swiss artist, who had been transplanted to England, strongly influenced the direction of English Romanticism.

When William Blake (1757–1827) said that 'the world of the imagination is the world of eternity', he defined succinctly the

47

33 WILLIAM BLAKE (1757–1827)
Songs of Innocence c. 1789

34 JOHN MARTIN (1789–185
Manfred on the Jungfrau 18

35 JOHN FLAXMAN (1755–1826)   *Thomas Chatterton Taking the Bowl of Poison from the Spirit of Despair*

36 WILLIAM BLAKE *Dante Meeting Beatrice in Paradise* 1824

essential peculiarity of his character and his art. A student of Chaucer, Milton and the Bible, Blake was a disciple of Boehme, Swedenborg and Paracelsus, who opened the gates of the occult to him. He learned Italian ten years before his death so that he could read Dante in the original. If his inexperience and ineptitude in the conduct of practical affairs were total, and his efforts to come to terms with them erratic, it was only because the invisible and the imaginary claimed him completely. His kingdom begins at the boundary of the worlds of other men.

We realize that his contemporaries could hardly have understood him, that they must have virtually condemned him to misery and that, thanks to his moody temperament, he had few protectors and few friends. And yet we are struck by the essential and profound honesty of an art which, while entirely devoted to the fantastic, depicts it with perfect objectivity. Blake's characters have a classic

7 JOHN MARTIN *Sadak in Search of the Waters of Oblivion* 1812

38   GEORGE ROMNEY (1734–1802)   *Nature Unveiling Herself to Shakespeare*   1786

beauty which relates them to those of Carstens and Flaxman, and a graphic purity which recalls Ingres. The hint of coldness in his figures is counter-balanced by the extraordinary movement which animates all his compositions (*Ills. 33, 36*): the interplay of curves and their equilibrium in the movements of these undulating forms represents an original cosmic energy. His line has an autonomous vitality, at once supple and extended like a musical phrase.

In this regard Blake is quite close to John Martin (1789–1854), but Martin was further removed from the Classical ideal by his intemperate disposition, which gave a touch of the fantastic to his paintings, mezzotints and illustrations for *Paradise Lost*. He was a believer in the bizarre, which he expressed with a capricious and fascinating genius (*Ill. 34*). He was a man of apocalyptic visions in which he dealt with actual episodes from ancient history: *Marius Meditating on the Ruins of Carthage* or *Sadak in Search of the Waters of Oblivion*, 1812 (*Ill. 37*) or the Miltonic combat between the infernal legions and the loyal angels. For Martin the endless halls of the underworld palace of Lucifer had the same architecture as the colonnades of Carthage: in their shadowy immensity the architectural perspectives, lit by thousands of torches, get lost in the distance.

Milton shares with Shakespeare the privilege of having vigorously influenced English Romantic painters. George Romney (1734–1802), the great portraitist, produced several dramatic compositions taken from Milton and Shakespeare (*Ill. 38*). But it was Shakespeare who furnished the richest and most tragic themes: the *King Lear in the Storm*, 1767 (*Ill. 39*) of John Runciman (1744–68) is one of the finest examples of 'pictorial Shakespeare', a phenomenon also to be seen in the work of Delacroix, Carstens, Koch and Fuseli. Richard Parkes Bonington (1801–28), one of the most scholarly and exquisite landscapists of the period (*Ills. 40, 41*), and one from whom the

39 JOHN RUNCIMAN (1744–68) *King Lear in the Storm* 1767

40 RICHARD PARKES BONINGTON (1801–28)
The Castelbarco Tomb, Verona 1827

41 RICHARD PARKES BONINGTON
The Institute Seen from the Quays, Paris

42 DAVID SCOTT (1806–49) *The Russians Burying their Dead* 1832

Romantics learned much, retained only the 'troubadour grace' of this 'Shakespearism'. An historical painter, he preferred to use episodes from the Renaissance or the Middle Ages, while David Scott (1806–49) displayed dramatic but measured vigour in his sober composition, *The Russians Burying their Dead* (*Ill. 42*).

John Copley (1737–1815) and Benjamin West (1738–1820), the distinguished narrative painters, belong to American rather than English history. Joseph Wright (1734–97), called Wright of Derby, who resembles Greuze in his subjects and in his way of treating them, is rather closer to the eighteenth century than to Romanticism (*Ill. 44*), even though his *Virgil's Tomb by Moonlight* (1779) seems to partake of the Romantic sensibility. But the work of these men— together with *Man Fighting a Sea Monster* (*Ill. 43*) by John Hamilton Mortimer (1741–79) and the paintings of Benjamin Haydon (1786– 1846), so much appreciated in his own time and so controversial today (*Ill. 45*)—is only the work of minor Romantics who belong to the second rank of Romanticism.

43 JOHN HAMILTON MORTIMER (1741–79)
Man Fighting a Sea Monster

44 JOSEPH WRIGHT (1734–97) *Experiment with an Air-pump* 1768

The animal portraitists who flourished in the seventeenth and eighteenth centuries, thanks to the well-known love of the English for their dogs and horses, are much more interesting though less well known. Although we may legitimately find Francis Barlow (1626–1702), James Seymour (1702–52) and John Wootton (c. 1678–1765) greatly interesting, it is only with the arrival of Romanticism that English animal portraiture inspires such excellent painters of horses as Sawrey Gilpin, 1733–1807 (*Ill. 49*), James Ward, 1769–1859 (*Ill. 48*) and George Stubbs, 1724–1806 (*Ill. 50*).

Stubbs' masterpiece is the set of three paintings showing a fight between a lion and a horse—painted, it is said, after he had seen such a fight during his trip to Morocco in 1755. The final scene was copied by Géricault, but the most gripping of the three is the

5   BENJAMIN HAYDON (1786–1846)   *Portrait of William Wordsworth*   1842

White Horse Frightened by a Lion (*Ill. 47*) which hangs in the Walker Art Gallery, Liverpool. The lion, crouching in the half-shadows, is a nocturnal creature, frightening and hellish. Threatened by the wild beast, the charger snorts and rears back, not so much frightened as seized by a kind of sacred horror. One recalls, too, Stubbs' enigmatic picture of two monkeys, *A Baboon and an Albino Macaque Monkey*, c. 1770 (*Ill. 46*): here the painter evidently wanted to express that moment when animality approaches human nature, imitating man's attitudes and gestures. In this strange canvas Stubbs, led by what Poe called the Angel of the Bizarre, surpassed the bounds of ordinary animal painting by a wide margin to reach into more mysterious zones of consciousness. Yet Ward almost equalled

46　GEORGE STUBBS (1724–1806)　*A Baboon and an Albino Macaque Monkey*

47   GEORGE STUBBS   *White Horse Frightened by a Lion*   1770

this achievement with his moving *Horse and Boa Constrictor* (1803)
and the splendid *Fall of Phaeton* (Lord Camrose's Collection).

Two equally powerful influences met at the source of English
landscape painting; one emanated directly from the nature of the
English countryside and its distinctive peculiarities, while the other
stemmed from the cult of Claude Lorrain among English enthusiasts.
Undoubtedly they would not have loved this painter so passionately
had they not perceived in his pictures a sensibility similar to their
own, and a conception of the sublime and the picturesque which
was embodied in the art of gardening long before it appeared in
painting.

It would be interesting to know to what extent and in what way Claude's pictures in English collections inspired the first landscape architects who proclaimed the revolt against topiary gardens and regimented alleys. It would be easy to believe that Chambers, Kent, Lancelot Brown and Whateley, and their aristocratic emulators Pitt, Walpole, Hamilton and Lyttleton, recognized that in Claude's pictures the elements of the sublime and the picturesque are in harmonious accord. Even when Richard Wilson (1714–82) went to paint Rome and its environs (*Ill. 52*) he carried with him a nostalgia which permeates his Italian landscapes and invests them with an English atmosphere. On his return to England this Welshman, who was unknown to the public and misjudged by connoisseurs, brought with him a certain Italian feeling. However, it was Claude's powerful and melodious harmony, from which Wilson learned so much, which helped to co-ordinate and animate Wilson's combination of Anglicisms and Italianisms.

The English landscape, like that of Claude, became a composition where reality is organized both musically and poetically, but here we

48 (left) JAMES WARD
(1769–1859)
*Bulls Fighting with View
of Donatt's Castle (Glams.)
in the Distance*

49 (above) SAWREY GILPIN
(1733–1807)
*A Road Horse
of the Duke of Cumberland*

50 (right) GEORGE STUBBS
A Skinned Horse c. 1776

51   RICHARD WILSON (1714–82)   *Cader Idris*   c. 1774

must distinguish between two separate tendencies. The first of these
is an attempt to perceive and to represent poetic reality as it is found
in the objective existence of things. To this group the first English
Romantics belong: Richard Wilson, John Crome, nicknamed Old
Crome, and the painters of the Norwich School who derive more or
less from him. The second group, which saw the landscape as a creation of a sympathetic, interpretative or imaginative fancy, accom-
modated temperaments and talents as diverse as Gainsborough and
Palmer, Constable and Turner. The first group put the accent on
objectivity; with the second, subjectivization could be so absolute
that it almost became, in Turner's work, a visionary surrealism, an
abstraction in which the subject of the painting disappears or
becomes unimportant.

RICHARD WILSON *Ruins of 'Maecenas' Villa' at Tivoli* c. 1765

53 JOHN CROME (1768–1821) *Mousehold Heath: Boy Tending Sheep* 1818–20

Old Crome (1768–1821) was undoubtedly closer to the Dutch
School than to Claude, both in theory and in temperament (*Ills. 53,
54*), but Ruysdael and Hobbema helped him primarily to discover
himself, and his best works, such as *The Poringland Oak, c.* 1818 (*Ill.
55*) and *Moonrise on the Yare* (*c.* 1808, National Gallery, London), are
those in which he resembles no one but himself. There is a quality
in these pictures which is not found in the work of Wilson, although
the latter achieved in his *Cader Idris, c.* 1774 (*Ill. 51*), an impressive
grandeur to which the more domestic Crome could not aspire. One
understands why Constable said that he remembered Wilson's
landscapes as 'delicious dreams'.

But we are still justified in asking, 'What is reality?', for so many
different ways seem to lead to it and to express it. At first glance one
would say that the landscapes of Thomas Gainsborough (1727–88)
undergo the same idealizing process as his portraits (*Ill. 58*): beginning

JOHN CROME *Landscape with Cottages*

55 JOHN CROME *Poringland Oak* *c.* 1818

6 THOMAS GAINSBOROUGH (1727–88) *The Market Cart* 1786

57   THOMAS STOTHARD (1755–1834)   *Greek Vintage*

with an objective perception, he seeks the essential character of a
place like that of a face, finding it dreamy, melancholy or moving,
reflecting his own emotion. He gives his sitters a rather fey grace
which transfigures them into something 'rich and rare', at once
supremely aristocratic, lyrical and romantic. But in painting landscapes he does not always follow nature: rather he constructs it, using
hallucinatory techniques like those of Leonardo da Vinci, the
Chinese painters or Hokusaï. Reynolds once told of having seen
extraordinarily small models in Gainsborough's studio, made of
blades of grass, lumps of moss, twigs, pebbles, fragments of mirrors.
Using these models, which probably served his imagination as a
starting-point, Gainsborough *invented* his landscapes.

68

58   THOMAS GAINSBOROUGH   *Study of a Lady* ▶

59 JOHN CONSTABLE (1776–1837) *Marine Parade and Chain Pier, Brighton* 1824

This process of exalting and transmuting reality, with the object as his basis, is typically Romantic. *The Market Cart*, 1786 (*Ill. 56*) and *The Bridge*, *c.* 1777, begin as 'impressions', emotions, but are developed and amplified; the minute elements of the model, resuscitating the emotion aroused by nature, are transformed into elemental forces. Thus the painted landscape vibrates more resonantly, and the little figures, which were moulded and placed in the model in the same positions that they would occupy in the picture, acquire a magical life. When we compare these figures with the animals with which James Ward (1769–1859) enlivened his paintings, we can measure Gainsborough's superiority in this respect, although Ward was a vigorous and brilliant colourist whom Géricault rightly admired. Ward had sympathy for the land: his palette glows with

60　JOHN CONSTABLE　*Weymouth Bay*　1816

deep, warm reds and vivid greens, and he could bathe his subjects with a blonde, golden light and a sumptuous radiance. His work has the same sensual quality which appears contemporaneously in the nudes of William Etty (1787-1849). These are warm and realistic, although perhaps a little heavy, and filled with a healthy and beautiful desire which does not always manifest itself in the work of Thomas Stothard (1755-1834). However, no one could equal Stothard in his treatment of the characters of antiquity and mythology, transposing them into an English park as mellow, lyrical figures which have that 'up-to-date' elegance and rather mannered grace of the women painted by Gainsborough (*Greek Vintage, Ill. 57*, for example, or *Nymphs Discover Narcissus*—both in the Tate Gallery).

It was no accident that John Constable (1776–1837) became a landscape painter. After a long struggle with his father, who refused to countenance his taking up a career as an artist, he began as a portraitist to satisfy his family, as they considered this at least more lucrative and perhaps more honourable. Certainly it won him more esteem (and more profit) from his contemporaries than did his landscapes, which most art lovers found disconcerting. As a result of his scrupulousness he was destined neither to add to nor subtract from the familiar aspects and the majesty of the English landscape as he saw it.

Constable's unwillingness to lose sight of anything which is there, and which, because it *is* there, ought to be grasped and appreciated, was accompanied by a kind of urgency. This can be seen in his sketches where the speed of execution, the swift touches limited to the precise and essential, attest to a wish to capture the very moment and embrace it completely. This urgency also accounts for the big difference between his sketches and the finished paintings. If we study, for example, the two *Hay Wains* (1821), the two *Salisbury Cathedrals*, 1823 (*Ill. 65*) or the two versions of *The Leaping Horse* (1825) the so-called rough draft is nothing of the sort: it is a completely finished work in itself and, in Constable's eyes, the equal of the finished picture—even superior to it, because the sketch is filled with the original emotion which drains away during work on the painting.

In this way the enthusiastic Romantic, working instinctively and guided only by the creative urge, sought to steady himself in his major compositions. Thus, while the sketches seem shaken by violent exterior and interior currents, and seem to be still in the making, as it were, the finished painting has a calm and grandiose monumentality (*Ills. 59, 60*). And when Constable was finally led to abandon his ruins to the bitter solitude of a haunted castle placed in a landscape shaken by storm, as in *Hadleigh Castle* (1829), the critics condemned it as madness. Since here objective vision borders on a visionary, fantastic, eminently Romantic creation, it became the butt of mockery and incomprehension.

Constable wrote of aiming at 'light—dews—breezes—bloom—and freshness; not one of which has yet been perfected on the canvas

72

61 JOHN CONSTABLE *Malvern Hall* 1809

by any painter in the world'. This avowal reveals as much pride as humility, coupled with an appreciation of the true value of every object. He is content with his interpreter's role, although he is probably unjust to the Dutch masters who preceded him and who had already discovered that 'the sky is the keynote, the standard of scale, the chief organ of sentiment'. Through his celebration of light, constantly changing and altering everything that it touches, he established it as something neither colourless nor transparent, but a very real entity. This realization of the material nature of light explains why he could also paint the corporeality of mists, and give his skies the significance of an element which is less fluid than compact. The humidity suspended in the atmosphere of the English countryside thus becomes perceptible and palpable, and one realizes what Fuseli meant when he said that seeing a picture by Constable made him want his umbrella and mackintosh.

62 JOSEPH MALLORD WILLIAM TURNER (1775–1851) *Appulia in Search of Appulius* 1814

Constable's peculiar sense of spatiality was first shown in *Malvern Hall*, 1809 (*Ill. 61*). Here it is not the immensity of the scene which matters. Nor is it in *The Dell in Helmingham Park* (1830, Tate Gallery, London), a crowded composition resembling a dragon's lair; in both cases it is the density of the area depicted which counts, an area in which every corner vibrates.

Little more than a year before Constable was born in a Suffolk farm-house, Joseph Mallord William Turner (1775–1851) was born at a London barber's near Covent Garden. He was apprenticed when very young to an engraver, and began by drawing the beautiful and romantic ruins of Gothic abbeys, such as Tintern Abbey and Malmesbury Abbey, and developing as he went an interest in the

63 JOSEPH MALLORD WILLIAM TURNER *The Parting of Hero and Leander* 1837

architectural problems which they posed. He was more open to the poetry of these ruins than was Constable, who declared that 'the feelings which guided their inventors are unknown to us' and who objected especially to the neo-medieval because 'a new Gothic building is in reality little less absurd than a new ruin'. Turner tasted the sumptuous melancholy of the Gothic arches in drawing their sinewy ogives against the sky. He also loved those paintings by Claude which inspired his own great compositions on Classical subjects (*Ill. 63*), such as *Appulia in Search of Appulius* (1814, National Gallery, *Ill. 62*), *Dido Building Carthage* (1815, National Gallery), *Dido and Aeneas* (1814, Tate Gallery), *Apollo and the Sibyl* (*c.* 1800, Tate Gallery), and *Agrippina Landing with the Ashes of Germanicus* (1839, Tate Gallery).

75

64   JOSEPH MALLORD WILLIAM TURNER   *Sun Rising through Vapour*   1807

And he also imitated Claude's sunsets over the sea, his ostentatious colonnades and his porticos open to the shore.

In the famous *Steamer in a Snowstorm*, 1842 (*Ill. 67*) or the earlier *Fire at Sea* (*Ill. 66*) we see how—at the moment when objects lose all substantiality and dissolve in iridescent mists, or in a sheet of rain scintillating with sunlight—Turner's forces dematerialize more and more, both plastically and pictorially, rejecting all weight and opacity to become those 'golden visions' which so enchanted Constable although they were foreign to his own theory.

Turner's stay in Venice in 1830 confirmed him in that quest which he had already undertaken in 1807 when he painted his *Sun Rising through Vapour* (National Gallery, *Ill. 64*). It was perfectly natural that, in order to translate these celebrations of the illusory and the veracious

JOSEPH MALLORD WILLIAM TURNER *Salisbury Cathedral: View from the Cloister*

66   JOSEPH MALLORD WILLIAM TURNER   *Fire at Sea*   *c.* 1834

on to canvas, Turner should increasingly turn to the most delicate, subtle and transparent mode of expression: the water-colour. Turner is above all a poet of light, who melts the world of reality and the world of appearances into an indissoluble harmony. His work is an incessant and bitter struggle between matter and spirit. His mistakes and his failures Ruskin attributed to 'his lack of faith and his despair'.

Water-colour technique, which preserves the hand's spontaneity with immediacy of vision and freshness in execution, became the favourite medium of those English artists who preferred this limpid material in which sensibility could reach the limits of emotion without ever coarsening it by retouching. Thus transposed into water-colour, the spirit of Keats and Shelley becomes pure poetry: such

67, 68   JOSEPH MALLORD WILLIAM TURNER   *Steamer in a Snowstorm*   1842 (above) ▶
Interior at Petworth   1837 (below)

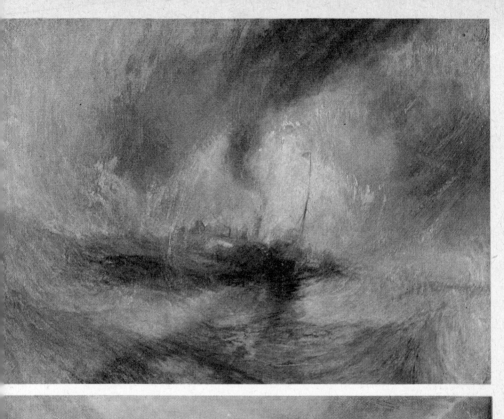

69 JOHN ROBERT COZENS (1752–99) *Valley of Zion*

Constable called the art of John R. Cozens (1752–99), who in his opinion was 'the greatest genius who ever painted landscapes' (*Ill. 69*). Cozens was a friend of William Beckford, the owner of Fonthill and author of *Vathek*, and travelled with him in Italy after studying under his father, who had published 'A New Method of Assisting the Invention in Drawing Original Compositions of Landscape' in which one finds several formulae of the kind employed by Gainsborough. Thomas Girtin (1775–1802) was a water-colourist to whom Turner paid tribute by saying that 'had he lived I should have starved'. Girtin's achievement lay in his ability to reconcile the fresh transparency of the water-colour with the substantial objectivity of the material, which in his work is not nullified by light, but acquires a new reality (*Ills. 70, 71*). David Cox (1783–1859) was originally a set-designer in Birmingham, and even his water-colours, sometimes executed like back-cloths, have a somewhat artificial grace (for example, *Terrace of Haddon Hall*, 1849, Ashmolean Museum, Oxford).

70 THOMAS GIRTIN (1775–1802) *Subject from 'Ossian'*

71 THOMAS GIRTIN *View on the Wharf, Farnley* c. 1800

72 (above) JOHN SELL COTMAN
(1782–1842)
Croyland Abbey 180...

73 JOHN SELL COTMAN
The Baggage Waggon 1828

74 SAMUEL PALMER (1805–81) *Coming From Evening Church* 1830

75 SAMUEL PALMER *Cornfield by Moonlight with the Evening Star*

To consider the work of John Sell Cotman (1782–1842) is to consider oils that have a rare quality of dramatic nobility (for example *The Baggage Waggon*, 1828, *Ill. 73*, or *After the Storm*, 1825, private collection, Norwich). Cotman's water-colours, on the other hand, were mostly done in his youth, and he abandoned this medium almost entirely around his thirtieth year. As for John Varley (1778–1842), who was a friend of William Blake and the teacher of Samuel Palmer, if he seems a coxcomb beside Girtin and Cozens he is nonetheless a skilful professional, inclined somewhat to virtuosity, but whose feelings bubble over in his purely technical exercises.

If with regard to the water-colourists we can talk of a Romanticism of the transcendent, then the Romanticism of that visionary Naturalist Samuel Palmer (1805–81) is the expression of the 'magic of matter' itself, of the mystery which dwells in the nature of things. *The Harvest Moon* (1835, Tate Gallery), *Coming from Evening Church*,

1830 (*Ill. 74*) and *Pastoral Scene* (1834, Ashmolean Museum, Oxford) transport the spectator into an unreal atmosphere or, rather, make him experience a reality other than that ordinarily perceived. The very original technique employed by Palmer, his mixing of oils and tempera, gives a unique texture to his pictures, which seem thick and grainy without suffering any loss of fluidity or transparency (*Ill. 75*). Unlike those artists who do their utmost to reproduce a particular landscape, he moves in an imaginary world where the other side of the reality of objects is shown in a peaceful and serene intimacy, where the full and deep atmosphere of the scene raises deep waves of a previously unheard harmony.

A steady whittling away of talent, a vulgarization of spirit and the decline of the great school of portraitists and landscapists, reaching its climax in Mulready (*Ill. 76*) and Wilkie's little genre paintings,

76 WILLIAM MULREADY (1786–1863) *The Seven Ages of Man* 1837

77 DANTE GABRIEL ROSSETTI (1828–82) · *The Wedding of St George and Princess Sabra* 1857

78 (opposite) WILLIAM HOLMAN HUNT (1827–1910)
Claudio and Isabella 1850

marked the end of English Romanticism. Yet it was a final outburst of the Romantic spirit which, eleven years after the death of Constable and three years before that of Turner, led to the foundation of the Pre-Raphaelite Brotherhood in 1848—if one can give the name Romantic to their desire to turn away from their own time, which they considered mediocre and banal, instead of trying to transform it and bring it back to its former glory. William Holman Hunt (1827–1910), Dante Gabriel Rossetti (1828–82) and Edward Burne-Jones (1833–98) adopted the same attitude of rejection as the Nazarenes, taking refuge in a land and a time which was not their own, adopting Italy and the Renaissance as an artistic and intellectual fatherland (*Ills. 77–9*).

They possess Romantic nostalgia, but without the intense communion with nature which inspired Constable, Friedrich and Rousseau. There is nonetheless something sincere and noble, even Romantic, about their revolt against the materialism and mechanization of the industrial age. And if they wanted their dreams to transport them to a world of pure and ingenuous beauty, of poetic grace and dreamy voluptuousness, their desire led them to found, according to Ruskin, 'the noblest school of art we have seen in the past three centuries'. William Morris (1834–96) achieved a more faithful and more efficacious return to the past in revitalizing serious decorative art, inspired by the Gothic but not copying it, and possessing a popular element which made it accessible to all.

Beside the pallid angels of Burne-Jones and the pensive beauties of Rossetti, the robust realism of Ford Madox Brown (1821–93) has a refreshing quality, although the quality of the painting is always subordinated to the subject. The plastic and pictorial aspects have less importance than the story which they tell. The great audacities of Constable and Turner have no successors; the Pre-Raphaelites, in confining themselves to the past, condemned themselves to an even narrower academicism than that of the Nazarenes since it was more systematic and held almost as a religion. Only George Frederick Watts (1817–1904) brought in a new element, since his work is so strongly contaminated by literature. Despite an excess of symbolism

79 EDWARD BURNE-JONES (1833–98) *Danaë and the Brazen Tower* 1872

and ideology, and a cult of 'great ideas' (which are not really neces-
sary in order to produce good paintings), Watts was more genuinely
dramatic and more authentically a poet than other contemporary
painters, with the exception of Samuel Palmer, the most admirable
of them all.

The Pre-Raphaelite Brotherhood, which was formed out of a desire
to return to the spirit of the Middle Ages and the Renaissance,
marked a strong reaction on the part of English sensibility against
the increasingly tyrannical despotism of the Industrial Revolution
and of the priority given to economic rather than intellectual or
spiritual matters. Fearing an even greater invasion by materialism,

the artists of the Brotherhood took refuge in dreams and nostalgia for the past and legendary worlds in order to escape the cruel harshness of the times so faithfully mirrored in Dickens' novels. They were encouraged in this flight by the warnings of John Ruskin, whose thought guided English aesthetics at the time. But Ruskin also foresaw the rise of a thorough study of nature, a patient observation of reality which would permit one to see beyond visible reality and so perceive the sublime mechanism of a universe created and ruled by God, discerning in the most humble objects the 'incessant working of the divine which embellishes and glorifies them'. The close attention to detail of William Holman Hunt (1827–1910), unlike the stormy symbolism of George Watts, defines precisely the smallest

80 FRANCIS DANBY (1793–1861) *Disappointed Love*

81   WILLIAM HOLMAN HUNT   *The Hireling Shepherd*   1851

blade of grass, as in *The Hireling Shepherd*, 1851 (*Ill. 81*), enabling the painter and the spectator to commune with the soul of the world in a kind of pantheistic wedding of the individual and the object.

The lessons given by the French Realist Legros at the Slade School in 1878 could have had the same effect in England as the showing in Munich in 1869 of Courbet's *Stone Breakers*, leading to a systematic and brutal Naturalism like that of Bastien-Lepage. But English art preferred, far above absolute objectivity, a poetic transmogrification of reality such as one finds even in narrative painting like the *Order of Release* (1853, National Gallery) by John Everett Millais (1829–96) as well as in a sentimental work like *Disappointed Love* (*Ill. 80*) by Francis Danby (1793–1861), or in the prettily and almost

82 FORD MADOX BROWN (1821–93) *The Baa-lambs* 1852

comically idyllic *Baa-lambs* (*Ill. 82*) by Ford Madox Brown, or the
too-well-known *Light of the World* (Keble College, Oxford) by
Holman Hunt. In these works art is at once delicately Naturalistic
and allusively symbolic.

The sentimentality in these pictures is both sincere and moving
because in each case the painter has been profoundly and sincerely
moved, and the feeling in them may be described as sentimental
realism. Yet often the banality of the theme and the wish to remain
in direct contact with the true nature of forms and deeds leads to a
'slice of life' product such as an illustration for a Dickens novel—for
example, *Omnibus Life in London*, 1859 (*Ill. 83*) by William Maw
Egley (1826–1916). Egley was born during Constable's lifetime and

83 WILLIAM MAW EGLEY (1826–1916) *Omnibus Life in London* 1859

yet lived to see the development of the first movements of the twentieth-century *avant-garde*: Cubism, Fauvism and Futurism. He was the son of a miniaturist and himself 'fussed' over details, whether a young girl's hat or a bouquet. Egley represents a character-istic facet of British Realism: discreet, reserved, modestly sentimental, and able to see the intimate poetry in those things whose beauty we no longer see because they are grown too familiar.

The search for the picturesque became more externalized, more independent of the feelings and, in a sense, more formal in Walter Greaves' painting. Greaves (1846–1931) knew Whistler and was strongly influenced by him. But he opposed the anti-Naturalism of the American painter, and clung to his own vision of the world,

93

84　WALTER GREAVES (1846–1931)　*Hammersmith Bridge on Boat-Race Day*　c. 1862

vivid, animated, amusing in his adroit treatment of details. *Hammersmith Bridge on Boat-Race Day, c.* 1862 (*Ill. 84*), a very typical example of Greaves' talent and wit, is an important landmark in the history of English Realism, since it is only three years later than Egley's *Omnibus* and twelve years later than *Christ in the House of His Parents* (*Ill. 85*) by Millais. There is nothing here of the sentimental picturesque of the style of Dickens or Egley, nor of the realistic style of Legros, who in any case did not arrive in London till much later; it is typically English in the brilliance of its colour and the amusingly droll poses; in its composition there is a very modern sense of the distribution of masses which, in its audacious stylization, almost foreshadows abstract art.

94

The essential English art of the portrait springs from the Renaissance in the miniatures of Hilliard and Oliver, and was especially brilliant in the eighteenth century. It found favour again among connoisseurs (whom Romanticism had inclined towards landscape rather than the human face) with the arrival of such different painters as John Singer Sargent, 1856–1925 (*Ill. 86*), Hubert Herkomer, Frank Holl (1845–88) and Sir William Quiller Orchardson (1835–1910). In landscape painting, however, the Romantic spirit had outstayed its welcome, until what novelty and fire was left had dried up. Two who remained unaffected by this decline were Cecil Gordon Lawson (1851–83), who died before his promise was fulfilled, and William Dyce, who was one of the most curious and attractive figures of English art of his time.

85   JOHN EVERETT MILLAIS (1829–96)   *Christ in the House of His Parents*   1850

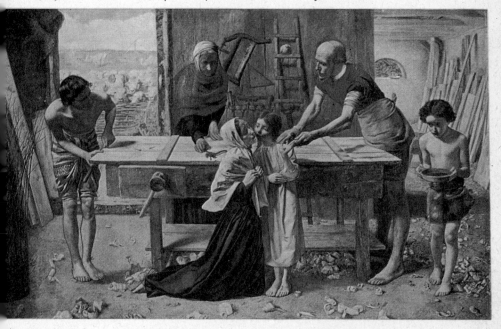

One cannot use the usual criteria in considering the peculiar quality of Dyce's Realism. He had worked in Italy, and while in Rome had been in contact with the Nazarenes. Later he bore heavy official duties which would have paralysed if not exhausted a less rich temperament. In the Tate Gallery there hangs one of his paintings which is almost unique not only in the English tradition but in all of nineteenth-century European art: at once simple and wise, it is perfect in execution and yet filled with an unequalled personal feeling. In *Pegwell Bay, Kent*, 1859–60 (*Ill. 87*) the artist has recalled and recorded exactly the emotions experienced on a precise date, 5th October 1858. The faces are portraits of his wife, his son and his

86   JOHN SINGER SARGENT (1856–1925)   *Repose*   1911

87   WILLIAM DYCE (1806–64)   *Pegwell Bay, Kent*   1859–60

sister-in-law, and Dyce has even remembered to reproduce Donati's comet in the sky, which appeared on that day. The landscape is treated with the same exact and affectionate attention to detail which he expends on the figures.

One could say that this picture is clumsily composed, while indicting the negligence of a 'photographer' who has portrayed the figures exactly as they presented themselves without considering the unity and harmony of the scene. Dyce's respect for objective reality was so great that he could no more modify the position of the persons than he could change the appearance of the cliffs of Pegwell Bay; his memories, probably reinforced by several rough sketches, create a work isolated and immobilized in time, eternalized by the attention and love which have retained the smallest details. But even

97

these are exalted by that kind of immortal beauty which the artist bestows upon his family, on the pebbles of the beach, on the distant strollers walking on the seaweed, or on the crystal-clear sky where the late afternoon light gives a curious feeling of waiting, of unease mingled with joy, of a calm solemnity which was for the artist the dominating emotion on this fifth of October which he has so magnificently perpetuated.

GERMANY

German Romanticism, while it is directly opposed to the ideals of the eighteenth century, artificially imposed by a small *élite* of thinkers who borrowed their ideas from French Rationalism and from the spirit of the Enlightenment, is immediately linked with a tradition which rejoins the great Germanic art of the fifteenth and sixteenth centuries. The discovery of the medieval texts of the 'Minnesängers' and the *Nibelungenlied* by the Swiss artist Bodmer, coupled with the work of Herder on folk poetry, created an unforeseen state of acceptance for these works of the past that the 'Aufklärung' (Enlightenment) had despised and ignored. Simultaneously, artists and thinkers returned to a direct experience of nature, to scientific and mystical study of the elemental world. Painters read the 'Naturphilosophen' and Carl Gustav Carus expressed, both in his paintings and in his writings as a philosopher and a Naturalist, the pantheistic conception of nature as Mother—nature intimately linked to the feelings of man. The painters rediscovered the Rhine, the 'German river' with its castles, cathedrals and little villages, unchanged since the Middle Ages.

Although the German Romantics repudiated Classicism, one of their first masters was the Danish painter Asmus Jacob Carstens, 1754–98 (*Ill. 189*) who, at a time when there existed a close artistic collaboration between Copenhagen and northern Germany, revealed a Romantic Classicism (or perhaps a Classicizing Romanticism) which followed the ideas expounded by Wehl in his book *The Beautiful in Painting*. Bonaventura Genelli (1796–1868), who followed Carstens, also tried to reconcile in his paintings the arbitrary paradoxes of Romanticism and Classicism. He borrowed eclectically

PATRIARCHAE
ET.
PROPHETA.

88 PETER VON CORNELIUS (1783–1867) *The Last Judgment (detail)*

from both medieval and Classical subjects, from Shakespeare, the idol of the German Romantics, and from Greek mythology.

Peter von Cornelius (1783–1867) and his fellow members of the *Lukas Bund*, the Guild of St Luke which settled in a Roman convent to paint and live a quasi-hermit life, brought about a revival of the great religious art of Germany (*Ill. 88*). This was more medieval than Baroque because the group we call the Nazarenes were trying to achieve a certain simplicity of approach and execution, a sobriety of lines and colours, and an almost naïve ingenuousness (although this

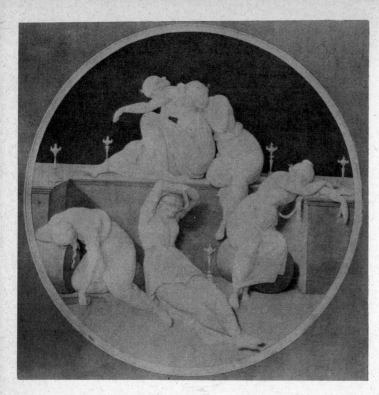

89 JOHANN FRIEDRICH
OVERBECK (1789–1869)
*The Wise and Foolish
Virgins*

naïvety was not always sincere). Today it is difficult to appreciate
the freshness of feeling which motivated their desire to return to the
humble and pious aesthetic of the 'primitives' (not the true primitives
but those painters who were so called at the time, the Italian and
German painters of the fifteenth century, including Raphael and
Dürer). The joyous outpourings associated with the resolution to
live a pure life for the sake of a pure art were the privilege of the
Nazarenes.

Johann Friedrich Overbeck (1789–1869) synthesized the ideal of
the Brotherhood, which he founded in Vienna in 1809 before
moving to Rome the following year, when he enunciated the law of
the 'three ways of art' which he himself had decided to follow: the
way of imagination, represented by Michelangelo, that of beauty,
represented by Raphael, and that of nature, represented by Dürer.
From the year 1810 the monastery of San Isidoro in Rome became
the meeting-place of those German painters who wished to lead a

religious life; Overbeck led the way by his conversion to Catholicism, an example which many followed. The patronage of the German consul Bartholdy and of Prince Massimo gave them the opportunity to execute vast murals with which they hoped to rival the illustrious fresco-painters of the Italian Renaissance. As well as Overbeck (*Ills. 89, 90*) and Cornelius there were a number of other talented painters; the first founders of the *Bund*—Wintegerst, Vogel, Hottonger, Sutter—who were soon eclipsed and are little known to posterity, followed by Wilhelm Schadow (1788–1862), Heinrich Maria von Hess (1798–1863), Johann Anton Ramboux (1790–1866), Schnorr von Carolsfeld (1794–1872), Carl Philipp Fohr (1795–1818), and the 'father of Romantic landscape painting', Joseph Anton Koch (1768–1839). Maria Alberti (1767–1810) is one of the most attractive personalities among these religious Romantic painters; she began by working in the manner of Pompeo Batoni and died nursing typhoid victims in a convent in Westphalia.

90 JOHANN FRIEDRICH OVERBECK *Joseph Telling His Dreams*

To what extent can we call the Nazarenes Romantics, since their declared ideal was to limit themselves to a strict imitation of the past's artistic forms, forms which their scruples would not permit them to change? The principal quality of their work is freshness: freshness of feeling, freshness of colour, the delicacy of the dawn, freedom of heart and of expression. With little effort and without set purpose they rediscovered the key to medieval simplicity because they strove for a simple heart and an ingenuous eye. Goethe misjudged them when he said that they were 'walking backwards, returning to the womb to create a new artistic era'. It is true that the Nazarenes made no technical progress towards modern painting, and that they would have arrested and even paralysed its evolution, but they are typical of one aspect of nostalgic German Romanticism. From them grew a new way of seeing and portraying the countryside, which the three Olivier brothers—Ferdinand, 1785–1841 (*Ill. 91*), Heinrich (1783–1848) and Friedrich (1791–1859)—learned from Koch.

Thanks to them, a new vision of landscape appeared in religious painting. No longer satisfied with simple Italianate settings, they placed episodes from the Old and New Testaments in the German countryside. The Jordan valley in *The Baptism of Christ* by Ferdinand and Heinrich Olivier (1808–10, in the parish church at Wörlitz) is as precisely rendered as if it had been painted in the sixteenth century by a member of the Danube School. The groupings of the angels and the watchers, unlike those of Overbeck or Cornelius, are not borrowed from Ghirlandaio or Perugino; they are treated with the realistic imagination, the picturesqueness and the animation we expect from the old masters of Swabia and Franconia.

Franz Pforr, who died in Albano at the age of twenty-four, was never tempted to forget his German background by the enticements of Italy. His *Entry of the Hapsburg Emperor Rudolph II into Basle* (1809–10, Städelsches Institut, Frankfurt-am-Main) preserves a rustic vigour, a simple, almost naïve feeling, and a robustness which have nothing to do with the theory of ideal beauty and Gothic Classicism cherished by the Nazarenes, who were intoxicated and blinded by the Italian Revolution. Carl Philipp Fohr, who drowned himself in

91 FERDINAND VON OLIVIER (1785–1841) *View of Salzburg* c. 1818

CARL PHILIPP FOHR (1795–1818) *Götz von Berlichingen Among the Gypsies*

the Tiber at the age of twenty-three, was the white hope of the new school; he had made a careful study of Cranach and Altdorfer, which he employed with romantic effect in his *Return from the Hunt* (Schloss Museum, Darmstadt). Hardly touched by the 'Italianizing' contagion, he preserved a robust feeling for reality (*Ill. 92*) which manifests itself principally in his portraits. One can recognize a German landscape in *The Vision of St Eustace* (Städelsches Institut, Frankfurt) by Johann David Passavant (1787–1861) who, before settling in the monastery of San Isidoro, had worked in Paris with David and Gros, while Ludwig Sigismund Ruhl (1794–1887) adopted the 'Troubadour genre', which is more artificial and more literary, in his *Fair Melusine at her Toilet* (Kunsthalle, Mannheim).

The old theme of the *danse macabre*, which formerly decorated so many churches and tombstones, was revived in the drawings of Alfred Rethel (1816–59). This artist, who painted enormous compositions telling the story of Charlemagne (Cathedral of Aix-la-Chapelle), was haunted by a world of phantoms and skeletons, an obsession which caused him to lose his reason when he was barely thirty-seven. He was deeply and essentially German like Schnorr von Carolsfeld, 1794–1872 (*Ill. 93*), who, although a Nazarene, no longer modelled himself on Fra Angelico or Raphael, but on the great German painter whom the Romantics fervently admired: Dürer. In composition and detail many of his paintings are, in spite of a surface Italianism, an act of homage to the perpetual and vigorous originality of the German master (*Ill. 93*).

The Viennese artist Moritz von Schwind (1804–71) maintained throughout his life a childish freshness of heart and mind. He believed in the legends of the forests and the Rhine and in the exploits of the paladins. Voluble, prolific, engendering the Austrian lightness of which he was the most delicate and subtle exponent (*Ill. 94*), he used the same palette for the idyll of *The Symphony* (Neue Pinakothek, Munich) as for the unreal marvels of enchanters and fairies. Like another Viennese, Eduard Jacob Steinle (1810–86), he rediscovered the capricious gaiety of the wandering scholars, of the Renaissance artists who made their journeys through a Germany of

93   SCHNORR VON CAROLSFELD (1794–1872)   *Siegfried and Kriemhilde*

gracious towns brimming with flowers, music and comradeship. One must rank with them, although they were better known as illustrators than as painters, the excellent Romantic engravers Eugen Napoleon Neureuther (1806–82) and Ludwig Adrian Richter, 1803–84 (*Ills. 95, 96*), the unforgettable poet of an ideal Germany, rustic and bourgeois with its dovecot-like houses, its forests haunted by gnomes and unicorns. But Richter is also—and this is far more significant—the creator of that painting, as melodious and romantic as a Schumann symphony, *Sailing on the Danube by the Schreckenstein* (1814, Dresden Gemäldegalerie). Here all the Romantic themes are united: the cliff crowned with ruins and gilded by the setting sun, the vagabond scholar, the musician and the pair of lovers.

94   MORITZ VON SCHWIND (1804-71)   *The Faithful Sister and the King's Son*

LUDWIG ADRIAN RICHTER (1803–84)
Geneviève de Brabant

96   LUDWIG ADRIAN RICHTER   *Peasants Returning from the Fields*

97 KARL SPITZWEG (1808–85)
The Outing

98 JOSEPH ANTC
KOCH (1768–183;
*Waterfalls near
Subiaco* 1813

This tender nostalgia, almost melancholy in its intensity, which we find in Schwind takes an ironic turn with Karl Spitzweg (1808–85). He discovered the poetry of Biedermeier Germany, the unromantic but touching episodes, and conferred on them a paradoxical beauty born of gentleness and an affectionate mockery (*Ill. 97*).

The evolution of the landscape in German Romantic painting, from picaresque or descriptive form to a lyricism where man and nature share the same emotional world and are rooted in a single being, may first be studied in the work of the Tyrolean Joseph Anton Koch (1768–1839). In his work we can greet the dawn of a new way of viewing and experiencing nature. Koch painted 'heroic pastorals' in the Italian manner and religious scenes in conventional settings, but he was also the first to see and to depict mountain scenery in a modern manner. Before settling in Rome, where he lived for forty-five years until his death, he had made careful and affectionate studies of the glaciers and waterfalls of the Bernese Oberland and of his native country (*Ill. 98*). But if he displays a certain clumsiness in painting scenes which no one before him had thought of depicting, and organizes his picture like an extended narrative with the details spread out verse by verse, as in a poem by Haller or Gessner, his feeling for nature is nonetheless very true, and his description retains the frankness of what he actually saw, of his experience.

Carl Gustav Carus (1789–1869), in his *Nine Letters on Landscape Painting*, expounded a more truly Romantic way of understanding and embracing nature than Koch's objective and analytic descriptions: 'Man, when he contemplates the magnificent unity of a natural landscape, is made conscious of his own insignificance and, feeling that everything is a part of God, he loses himself in the Infinite and renounces his individual existence. To bury oneself thus is no loss, it is a gain; what one can ordinarily see only through the spirit

99 CARL GUSTAV CARUS (1789–1869) *Allegory on the Death of Goethe* 1832

100   CARL GUSTAV CARUS   *Gothic Cathedral Seen through Ruins*   1832

almost becomes visible to the naked eye; one is convinced of the unity of the infinite universe'. This philosopher, who became a painter thanks to the influence and lessons of Friedrich, learned to express—in his paintings of the night, fog on pools, clouds enveloping mountains—the mysterious world where every echo and resonance, every intuitive interpenetration of man and the elements, plays in unison like the well-tuned instruments of an orchestra (*Ills. 99, 100*).

Caspar David Friedrich (1774–1840) towers above all other German painters of his time because he gives visionary pantheism its most beautiful and most varied forms of expression. His brilliantly precise drawings show that he observed nature not only with patient care but with an almost photographic exactitude which seizes on the individuality of a tree, because both tree and branch are

111

101 (opposite, above) CASPAR DAVID FRIEDRICH (1774–1840)
Mountain Landscape with Rainbow *c.* 1809

102 (opposite, below) CASPAR DAVID FRIEDRICH
Man and Woman Gazing at the Moon 1819

103 (above) CASPAR DAVID FRIEDRICH *The Cross and the Cathedral in the Mountains* *c.* 1811

living entities. The artist examines them in order to learn the secret of those organic structures which create and maintain life. His love of all things confers an intimacy which abolishes the arbitrary distinctions between the self and the non-self. For the Romantic everything is integrated in the self of the artist, everything emanates from him as a continuous osmosis is established between man and the universal flux in which he feels that he is rooted.

In each of Friedrich's paintings, whether it is the *Mountain Landscape with Rainbow* (c. 1809, Folkwang Museum, Essen, *Ill. 101*), *A Monk beside the Sea* (Berlin) or *Man and Woman Gazing at the Moon* (1819, Nationalgalerie, Berlin, *Ill. 102*), contemplation is action. It is the movement of the soul towards inanimate objects and the opposite journey of these objects, which are in turn assimilated by the painter. When Friedrich advised the artist, 'Shut the physical eye in order to see your subject first with the spirit's eye, then steer towards the daylight that you have perceived among the shadows', he defined the essentially Romantic process of creation where representation of a real, exterior and objective landscape becomes at the same time a transcription of the images which dwell in the conscious and subconscious of the painter. The process is the same whether the artist finds the presence of God in a cross standing on the mountainside as in the *Cross at Teschen* (1806, Berlin) or *The Cross and the Cathedral in the Mountains* (c. 1811, Düsseldorf, *Ill. 103*), whether he explores the ruins of a convent or a Gothic cathedral, or whether he experiences—perhaps before the infinity of the North Sea, perhaps in a thick pine forest—that communion with the holy which gives to all his subjects an intensely religious character. It begins with that conception of the universal soul equally present in all things which was the mark of the German mystics from Meister Eckhardt to Angelus Silesius and Böhme, and of poets such as Novalis and Hölderlin.

Friedrich's radiance was certainly that of his period. Not only did Gerhard von Kügelgen (1772–1820), Ferdinand Hartmann (1774–1842), Georg Friedrich Kersting, 1785–1847 (*Ill. 104*) and the Riepenhausen brothers (his pupils) spread and carry on the teaching of the master; the visionary pantheism of these Romantics was prolonged in

104
GEORG FRIEDRICH KERSTING
(1785–1847)
*Portrait of
Caspar David Friedrich
in His Studio* c. 1811

such post-Romantics as Marées and Böcklin, and more clearly in the Expressionist landscapes by Heckel, Kirchner and Nolde. And there is not a line by Friedrich that Paul Klee would not have been happy to endorse.

The names of two painters who are hardly known outside Germany stand out from the body of Romantic landscape painters, thanks to their affinities with the 'Naturphilosophen' and to their imaginative powers which link them directly to Friedrich. First, there is the very original Ernst Ferdinand Oehme (1797–1855), whose *Cathedral in Winter* (Dresden, Gemäldegalerie) combines the most striking Romantic themes: high Gothic spires and naves, dead trees, snow and the dark, and strange lights shining behind great windows; secondly, there is Carl Blechen (1798–1840), who painted

105　CARL BLECHEN (1798–1840)　*Iron Foundry at Neustadt-Eberswalde　c.* 1832

the Romantic masterpiece *Thunderbolt Striking A Coach* which was unhappily lost in the Crystal Palace disaster at Munich in 1931. Whereas Delacroix wanted to paint the flash of a sword, Blechen attempted a concrete representation of the murderous thunderbolt enveloped with a tragic grandeur, thus making it the instrument of a daemonic or divine Fate.

Blechen (*Ill. 105*) first worked as a scene-painter under the direction of Karl Friedrich Schinkel (1781–1841). Schinkel was also an architect, and a passionate devotee of that cult of the antique which littered Germany with pastiches of the Parthenon and classical porticos. As a painter he adored the Gothic (*Ill. 106*), and his best paintings show medieval cities dominating the bends of imposing rivers

106   KARL FRIEDRICH SCHINKEL (1781–1841)   *The Castle of the Grail*

and surmounted by the spires and bell-towers of fantastic cathedrals.

The very exceptional beauty of the work of these masters of tragic landscape increases the risk that the work of the minor Romantic masters may go unnoticed. Austria, for example, produced such sensitive and inspired interpreters of the friendly countryside around Vienna as Ferdinand Georg Waldmuller (1793–1865) and Adalbert Stifter (1805–68), who was famous as a novelist as well as a painter; the Prater and the Vienna woods do not possess the majesty and mystery of the forests visited by Friedrich, Carus, Oehme or Blechen, but these Austrians employ an easy and often moving grace to describe the simple and aristocratic charm of the Biedermeier period in the Hapsburg capital.

117

107   PHILIPP OTTO RUNGE (1777–1810)   *Rest on the Flight into Egypt*   1805–06

The desire to commune with nature, to efface one's individuality in the currents of cosmic energy, makes the portrait less important in the Romantic period than it had been in the eighteenth century. However, in the most outstanding portraits of the time—by Erwin Speckter, Victor Emil Janssen, Overbeck and Sigismund Ruhl— one finds a search for the hidden personality of the sitter. The painter does not limit himself to the public aspect, which is superimposed like a mask on the real traits of character, but questions any unease which he finds in his sitter, any melancholy and longing which may mark his face.

118

108 PHILIPP OTTO
RUNGE
*The Hülsenbeck
Children*
1805–06

109 PHILIPP OTTO
RUNGE
We Three
1805

110   HANS THOMA (1839–1924)   *In the Sun*   1867

Philipp Otto Runge (1777–1810) painted two of the most moving portraits in *We Three*, 1805 (*Ill. 109*) and *The Hülsenbeck Children*, 1805–6 (*Ill. 108*) and his many self-portraits are strongly representative of a vigorous and subtle realization of an interior world which brims out on to the canvas and there forms a moving landscape of flesh and bone. Runge was not only a portraitist; he was in love with everything in the universe and in his works depicted the hours of the day with allegorical figures representing trees and flowers. He planned that his immense compositions—which his premature death at thirty-three left unfinished—should be assembled in a kind of sanctuary where they could be viewed to the accompaniment of music and poems, to achieve that 'total work of art' which was the ideal of so many Romantics.

111
HANS THOMA
Boys Fighting
1872

Since Romanticism appeared after the flowering of the Middle Ages and seems one of the constants of the German genius, manifesting itself in its periodic resurgences by different outward 'signs' but always rising from the same essential spirit, it is as difficult to say when it disappeared from German art as it is to determine the precise moment of its breakthrough. Take the artists of the second half of the nineteenth century, in whose work the Romantic ideal is diluted and combined with the diverse tendencies of Realism and symbolism, artists such as Böcklin, Klinger, Hans von Marées or Anselm Feuerbach: should we consider them as Romantics or post-Romantics? Is not Lovis Corinth a modern master of Romantic landscape?

Certainly the characteristic trends of Romanticism were continued in the simple and tender landscapes of Hans Thoma, 1839–1924 (*Ills. 110, 111*) and Karl Haider, 1846–1912 (*Ill. 112*), a pupil of Ludwig Richter; in the romantic and tragic compositions of Arnold Böcklin

112   KARL HAIDER
(1846–1912)
Spring

113 ANSELM FEUERBACH
(1829–80)
Nanna 1861

(1827–1901), which were inspired by the artist's feeling of oneness with nature (*Ill. 114*); in the scenes of Anselm Feuerbach (1829–80), where antiquity is revived with a modern air (*Ill. 113*); and in the fantastic engravings of Max Klinger (1857–1920), who wavered between the Naturalistic 'slice of life', polychrome sculpture and the visionary resources of the engraver's tools.

Romanticism gave birth to new modes of expression and new ways of thinking and feeling, quite different from those of the preceding generations, in the work of Albert Welti (1862–1912), a Swiss who peopled the mountains of his country with devils, spectres and hobgoblins. This new sensibility is also apparent in the work of Hans von Marées (1837–87), a lyrical evoker of an antiquity bathed in the primeval spirit of the old German forests (*Ill. 115*), or in the work of the Austrian Gustav Klimt, and in Giovanni Segantini, 1858–99 (*Ill. 116*), the recluse of Majola, for whom the mountains had a living being which breathed in the Mediterranean silence. These tendencies, though so different, are no less Romantic in essence and form.

114 ARNOLD BÖCKLIN (1827–1901) *The Isle of the Dead* 1880

The cases of Hans Thoma and Karl Spitzweg have already shown
how artificial are divisions into categories and schools when discussing artists who cannot be fitted into narrow and arbitrary definitions.
The German Romantics explored the world of dreams, fancy and
imagination in order to discover a new reality, whereas the Realists
attempted a poetic transcription of nature which was at the same
time an enlargement of feeling and a deepening of emotion. This
desire to express the hidden poetry of everyday things is a genuine
national tradition, already recognizable in the work of Dürer, and
the influence exercised by Courbet and Millet on German Realism
was as much a result of their lyricism as of their *verisme*. And the joy
experienced by Courbet when he saw how well he was appreciated
after his 1869 show in Munich was only increased by the pride with
which this democratic 'revolutionary' received the Order of St
Michael from the King of Bavaria.

124

This 'plunge into reality' proposed by Courbet and Millet was a tremendous lesson for the German artists who were trying to find a way out of the academicism and Romanticism which had outlived its usefulness and was hindering art and making it anaemic. It is impossible to say where German Romanticism reached its apex, because a Romantic constant is present at all times after the Middle Ages, and one which does not oppose fidelity to reality. In the work of Richter or Schwind we see an attempt, elsewhere perfectly realized, to reconcile the dream and experience, to marry reality and fantasy. This attempt leads at times to a surreality comparable to some of the trends of Surrealism which today attempts to stick to reality and thus draw more power and brilliance from it than it could from the pure state of dreaming.

A homely, down-to-earth spirit marks one characteristic difference from the lyrical realism of the Romantics. This new quality of

115 HANS VON MARÉES (1837–87) *Diana Bathing* 1863

116   GIOVANNI SEGANTINI (1858–99)   *Angel of Life*

emotion was introduced by Courbet's *Stone Breakers* and appraised thus in an 1870 number of the *Zeitschrift für bildende Kunst*: 'Social problems have entered the widely opened doors of art.' However, social problems did not present themselves so sharply in Germany as in France, where the revolution of 1848 had left its mark (an unimportant episode as far as the Germans were concerned) and where there would shortly be the tragic experience of the Paris Commune. Although social questions in Germany did not take the aggressive and partisan form in which Courbet stated them, and although they never culminated in revolution, they nonetheless reflected the profound upheaval in Germany brought about by the arrival of the

126

industrial era, accompanied by a general enthusiasm for material progress and economic prosperity. It is significant that Adolf Menzel, who, with his flute recitals and little suppers, re-created the delights of Sans Souci for Frederick II, had by 1876 become a painter of factories. Menzel, 1815–1905 (*Ill. 117*) had shown a vital sense of observation and irony in his genre painting. He played for late nineteenth-century society the role that Chodowiecki took for eighteenth-century aristocratic society. But his chief interest, when he abandoned Potsdam, was the graceful good nature of the greedy and social-climbing middle classes of the German Empire. Menzel is truthful without being platitudinous, and instead of idealizing his subject he envelops it with the virtuosity of an elegant and scintillating technique in which can be seen the first flickers of Impressionism.

In the work of Wilhelm Leibl (1844–1900), on the other hand, the worldly and brilliant aspect which was dear to Menzel becomes a simple, grave objectivity. The one treasured movement, the other composed static figures, rather heavily monumental yet powerful

117 ADOLF MENZEL
(1815–1905)
Room with Open Window
1845

118 (above) WILHELM LE
(1844-190
The Spinning Wheel 18

119 (left) WILHELM TRÜBNER
(1851-1917)
Young Girl with Folded Hands
1878

120 (opposite) WILHELM LE
Three Women at Chu
1

121 FRITZ SCHIDER (1846–99) *The Leibl Family at Christmas* 1874

and serene. Leibl was a pupil of the narrative painter Piloty when he first saw the *Stone Breakers*, and his admiration for Courbet increased after seeing the artist again in Paris in 1869–70. He had a grandiose feeling for reality which endows his portraits, whether of peasants or aristocratic ladies, with a tranquil and composed dignity (and not a little solemnity). The famous *Cocotte* (Wallraf-Richartz Museum, Cologne) painted in Paris in 1869 is really an anecdote in the 'Paris manner', but the *Three Women at Church*, 1882 (*Ill. 120*) and the *Portrait of Rosine Treuberg* (1878, Vienna) are the best examples of his 'grand style', which is both forceful and considered. This was Leibl's cardinal virtue, which the painters of his circle tried vainly to equal. Wilhelm Trübner (1851–1917) is the closest of them to his master and, like him, was strongly influenced by Courbet. In his portraits, as for example *Young Girl with Folded Hands*, 1878 (*Ill. 119*), and his landscapes he attempted to rejoin the cult of a reality freed of all vulgarity, and to rediscover the very essence of the 'true' in his efforts to include all the atmosphere surrounding and animating material objects. Fritz Schider, 1846–99 (*Ill. 121*), Rudolf Hirth du Frênes, 1846–1916 (*Ill. 122*) and Louis Eysen (1843–99) all exhibit the same ideal; the transition from Courbet's influence to that of Manet and Degas is accomplished in their work, but without taming their robust originality. This originality was sustained by a sincere and intimate love of nature, which we find again in the paintings of Johann Sperl (1840–1914) and Carl Schuch (1846–1903), who was tempted by the Italian Picturesque but never escaped from the contagion of genre painting in the manner of Meissonier, which, in his blind predilection for anything coming from France, he valued too highly.

122 RUDOLF HIRTH DU FRÊNES
(1846–1916)
Leibl and Sperl in a Boat
· 1875

Despite his virtuosity as a portraitist, the realism of Franz Seraph von Lenbach (1836–1904) slides into academicism (*Ill. 123*), and it is not until the arrival of Max Liebermann (1847–1935) that one reaches a frank and airy representation of nature, open to feeling and to the *impression*. If Liebermann is not, properly speaking, an Impressionist, he at least showed the way to a form of expression which had not yet appeared in German landscape painting. And it was a form of expression which, unlike that of the group known as 'Die Scholle', was not subordinated to social justice-seeking or moralizing purposes. Nor does one see in Liebermann's paintings the kind of symbolic Realism which characterized the Worpswede Group.

Unlike Liebermann, Fritz von Uhde (1848–1911) falls into a kind of Naturalism which also appeared in France and which consisted of modernizing and bringing up to date certain episodes from the Old and New Testaments, by giving the characters costumes and settings of the painter's own time. This freak phenomenon corresponded to a desire to popularize religion, to show that in every age the same events recur in the same pattern. Fritz von Uhde made this transposition in his *Jesus in a Peasant Household* and in *Pilgrims to Emmaus*, showing the socialist Christian side of the Redeemer of the humble and meek, the 'God of the poor people', which coincided with those religious currents active in the second half of the nineteenth century that tried to bring together the Church and the masses. Public opinion, accustomed to a completely idealized version of Scriptural characters, was scandalized at the sight of the Apostles at the Last Supper travestied as a 'band of brigands', to use the words of a contemporary critic. Of course they were forgetting that during the Renaissance the Apostles were dressed like companions of the Medici or the Fuggers or the great merchant-bankers of Antwerp. Later, in the work of Permeke and his comrades in the Laethem St Martin Group in Belgium, there was a similar attempt to disguise the Apostles as peasants so that the peasants themselves could feel that they were both spiritually and materially closer to them.

An analogous Naturalism inspired the religious scenes of Max Klinger (1857–1920). This original and powerful artist pioneered the use of polychrome sculpture in Germany, creating strange and

123 FRANZ SERAPH VON LENBACH (1836–1904) *The Little Shepherd* 1860

fantastic carvings. In his pictures he pursued the same campaign as Fritz von Uhde towards democratization of religious representation. He extended Realism into the most violent and brutal Naturalism in his different portrayals of the Crucifixion, the strangest and most striking example of which is to be found at Leipzig. Every face is a portrait, and the smallest detail is selected and treated in a manner which suggests to the spectator that the artist is presenting an everyday happening, an item in the news, which he happened to witness.

The wave of religious Naturalism lasted long enough to appear in some of the works of Lovis Corinth (1858–1925), whose overpowering *Descent from the Cross* at Leipzig marks the beginning of a transitional stage between the Realism which this work proclaims and the Expressionism of which he was later to become one of the most brilliant and vigorous initiators. Expressionism in all its brutality and crudity is an idealization of reality, but the revolt against academicism and the banality sanctified by bourgeois taste had already begun with Realism. In truth, one could say that Romanticism in Germany—which was in its own way Realistic, since its aspirations were in accord with the Biedermeier spirit, as in the work of Spitzweg, Richter or even Schwind—prepared the way for a Naturalism which was often as artificial as the most arbitrary Romanticism. However, unlike the French Romanticism incarnated by Bastien-Lepage, German art was rarely content with a photographically exact representation of forms or a banality of feeling. It sought a spiritual element, which may at times be difficult to recognize, but to which the religious art of Klinger and Uhde bears eloquent testimony.

FRANCE

French architecture after the inspired and imaginative outburst of Ledoux's work lapsed into imitations and triviality. French painting, however, turned its spirit of restless inquiry, born of a feverish and sharpened sensibility and its love of the new pictorial media, to understanding and interpreting the period of upheavals from the fall of the monarchy to the establishment of the Commune. Although such eighteenth-century painters as Chardin, Watteau and Fragonard attached little importance to political events in Europe, the typical Romantic painter—whether David or Courbet or Daumier—is a seismograph recording all the little disturbances which agitate both society and the individual conscience. The Romantic painter is truly a 'man of his time' because the events which occur around him awaken a resonant echo in him. And thus it would be wrong to consider the artist in isolation from his time, for he is generally very deeply involved in its events. This is especially true of the Imperial epoch, which presented to the artist themes of diverse and moving grandeur.

If Napoleon paid little attention to the artistic movements of his day, he nonetheless dictated their direction in the pathos of their subjects provided by the Imperial wars. David himself lent his neo-Classicism to a courtly Realism in depicting contemporary events.

134

125 ANTOINE JEAN GROS *Napoleon Visiting Victims of the Plague at Jaffa* 1804

ANTOINE JEAN GROS (1771–1835)   *The Battle of Eylau*   1808

126   ANTOINE JEAN GROS   *Napoleon Crossing the Bridge at Arcola (detail)*   1796

127   ANNE-LOUIS GIRODET DE ROUCY-TRIOSON (1767–1824)   *The Funeral of Atala*   1808

As a result, the *Coronation of Napoleon* (1805, Louvre) is a magnificent illustration of contemporary history.

Very different artists were united in adulation of Napoleon. The most remarkable and the only inspired priest of the sun-myth was Baron Gros (1771–1835). In his *Napoleon Visiting Victims of the Plague at Jaffa* (1804, Louvre, *Ill. 125*), *Napoleon Crossing the Bridge at Arcola*, 1796 (*Ill. 126*) or *The Battle of Eylau* (1808, Louvre, *Ill. 124*), of which Napoleon is the hero, the leader is portrayed as a super-human figure whose very gesture can command men and almost overrule the elements.

Gros was trained in David's studio, and the teacher claimed to have retained influence over his pupil long after he had grown away from him and was justly rated as the 'most illustrious dissident' from

137

128 ANNE-LOUIS GIRODET DE ROUCY-TRIOSON
The Shades of French Warriors . . . 1801

David's school. Gros' lyrical temperament and richness of imagination could transfigure reality, making it impossible for him to be
confined by a strict, Classical Realism.

Compared with Gros, the painters who were inspired by the
Imperial campaigns seem chroniclers, even anecdotists. Anne-Louis
Girodet de Roucy-Trioson (1767–1824) took an episode from the
Egyptian campaign for *Revolt at Cairo*, but how different it is from
Napoleon Visiting Victims of the Plague at Jaffa. Girodet had turned
away from the Davidian Classicism of his youth in favour of the neo-
Gothic, almost the 'troubadour', and under the influence of Chateau-
briand painted *The Funeral of Atala*, 1808 (*Ill. 127*). Yet he too was an
interpreter of the Napoleonic myth in the bizarre composition which

129 JEAN AUGUSTE DOMINIQUE INGRES (1780–1867)
Study for 'The Dream of Ossian' 1866

he painted in 1801 for Malmaison. His love of reading Macpherson may have betrayed him into attempting to paint (and to name) that unlikely scene, *The Shades of French Warriors, Having Been Led by Victory into the Palace of Odin, Are Received by the Homer of the North and the Warlike Ghosts of Fingal and his Descendants* (*Ill. 128*).

François Gérard (1770–1831) painted Classical subjects, yet his painting in the Musée de Lyon, *Corinne at Miseno* (1819, inspired by Madame de Staël's famous novel), makes his claim to true Romantic inspiration and lyricism.

The almost unknown Boissard de Boisdenier (1813–66) is much more interesting. His admirable *Episode on the Retreat from Russia* (*Ill. 130*), painted in 1835, now hangs in the Musée de Rouen. Another

139

episode from the retreat from Moscow, painted by Charlet (*Ill. 131*) a year after Boisdenier's work, must be mentioned among the major Romantic works which incorporate the Napoleonic legend. Raffet (1804–60) is generally considered to be the Béranger of painting, the humorist and gossip-writer of the Imperial years (*Ill. 132*). He was a man who had shared the sufferings and the military glories of the veterans of the Old Guard, not as a 'H.Q. painter' like Gros, but as the comrade of the foot-soldiers, the torch of the rank and file, the hagiographer of the 'little flowers' of the Grande Armée.

When Jean Auguste Dominique Ingres (1780–1867) conceived the decoration of Napoleon's bedroom in the Quirinal with a *Dream of Ossian* (*Ill. 129*), by evoking ghosts he became a Romantic. The fantasy and prophetic atmosphere of this work make it one of the outstanding Romantic masterpieces—much more Romantic than such pictures in the 'troubadour genre' as *Paolo and Francesca* which are tiresomely 'period'.

130 BOISSARD DE BOISDENIER (1813–66) *Episode on the Retreat from Russia* 1835

131   NICOLAS TOUSSAINT CHARLET (1792–1845)   *The Retreat from Russia*   1836

132   DENIS AUGUSTE MARIE RAFFET (1804–60)   *La Revue Nocturne*   1834

133 JEAN AUGUSTE DOMINIQUE INGRES
Portrait of Granet 1807

134 (opposite)
EUGÈNE DELACROIX (1798–1863)
Greece Expiring on the Ruins
of Missolonghi 1827

Is it fair to call Ingres a Romantic? Contemporary critics, in particular David's supporters, were not far from thinking him Romantic when in 1806 they decided that his *Portrait of Madame Rivière* (Louvre) was 'bizarre, revolutionary and Gothic'. Certainly those are not the terms we would use today to describe a work which seems to our eyes rather guarded and not very revolutionary. In fact this painter, who believed that there was something rather animal about colour while line was essentially spiritual, was probably the closest of his contemporaries to the German Nazarenes, who shared his 'linear' prejudice (*Ill. 133*).

Baudelaire, whose poetic vision enabled him to see farther than the critics, detected affinities between Ingres and Courbet, a connection which would have astonished the Classicists as much as the Romantics. An unwarned and impartial student of Ingres must be struck by the contrast between forms which are meant to be Roman and 'Raphaelesque' and those of an interior Romanticism, a Romantic temperament which he felt obliged to subdue and repress. A conflict raged between the impulses of his artistic nature and human instincts on the one hand, and on the other his desire to be Classical, which was no less violent and painful for being suppressed.

135 EUGÈNE DELACROIX *The Massacre at Chios* 1824

EUGÈNE DELACROIX *The Abduction of Rebecca* 1846

Eugène Delacroix (1798–1863) defined his standpoint quite explicitly when he wrote in his diary: 'If one means by my Romanticism the free expression of my personal impressions, my remoteness from the groups which are inevitably fossilized into schools, and my repugnance for academic formulae, then I must say that I am a Romantic.' Elsewhere he said that 'the most beautiful works of art are those that express the pure imagination of the artist'. His principal contributions to the gospel of Romanticism are a horror of ready-made formulae in pictorial technique, in aesthetics or in inspiration (which he leaves in large part to the imagination and to the impression of a moment) combined with a quest for the harmonies of colour, and the notion of renewing emotion at the very places where the dramatic events of his time occurred, as in *Liberty Leading the People* (*Ill. 138*), *The Massacre at Chios* (*Ill. 135*) and *Greece Expiring on the Ruins of Missolonghi* (*Ill. 134*). One must add that he opened wide his mind and heart to poetry and music—he was an admirer of Byron and Berlioz—and sought in his painting that synthesis of all the arts which the German Romantics also pursued (*Ills. 136–8*). It is hardly astonishing, then, that Baudelaire saw him as 'a volcanic crater

137 EUGÈNE DELACROIX
The Death of Sardanapalus
(*detail*)
1827

138   EUGÈNE DELACROIX   *Liberty Leading the People*   1830

hidden by bunches of flowers', just as Schumann defined Chopin as 'a cannon under roses'.

Paul Delaroche (1797–1853), the idol of contemporary art-lovers, was preferred to Delacroix in his own lifetime. He has since been described as 'a mediocrity of the first order'. If Delacroix brought Romanticism to the point of Classicism, Delaroche, who lacked neither skill nor talent, led it back into academicism. By this I do not mean to exclude from Romanticism the painter of the *Children of Edward* (1831), *The Execution of Lady Jane Grey* (1834) and *The Death of Elizabeth* (1827)—subjects which prompted Heine's caustic observation that 'M. Delaroche is the painter of Their Decapitated Majesties'—but I do want to see this theatrical and emphatic painter placed in proper perspective.

Delacroix was a highly cultivated artist who instinctively sought inspiration wherever he might find it, and was blessed with a sense of judgment as perceptive as it was free from dogmatism. He never viewed his Romanticism as a potential weapon. The tumultuous frenzy of his genius was always controlled by a rigorous spatial concentration; and his indefatigable studies are attested to by the rhythms of the intersecting and entwining curves of *The Death of Sardanapalus* (1827, Louvre, *Ill. 137*), by the tumultuous movement which converges towards the centre of intense drama in *Liberty Leading the People* (1830, Louvre, *Ill. 138*), and by the ceiling of the Galerie d'Apollon in the Louvre, where he showed himself the equal of such great Baroque decorators as Maulbertsch and Tiepolo.

By his use of colour he rivals, and even surpasses, the musician as a creator of harmony. ('Colours are the music of the eyes. . . . Certain harmonies of colour produce sensations which music itself cannot achieve. . . .') He modulates brightness and intensity with the confidence of one who knows that form is born of colour and receives its life from it. With his sovereign ease in the handling of light and in the treatment of 'shadow light', his brush, which seems infused with light, picks out a solitary beam of sunlight, the brief brilliance of a reflection, the sumptuousness of iridescent cloth, the warm ambers and the pale ivories of moist skin; he makes the object and its reflection mirror each other, and they amalgamate in such a way that their complex reality seems like the confusion between dreams and the waking state.

Among the lesser Romantics who lack both fame and genius, perhaps because they were more Romantic in their lives than in their art, looms that strange personality known as Monsieur Auguste. He was one of Delacroix's intimates, and emerged in his wake. Jules Robert Auguste (*c.* 1789–1850) was a rather mysterious figure; the son of a rich jeweller, he was a sculptor, a horse-lover and a connoisseur of eighteenth-century painting at a time when public taste abominated the Rococo in reaction against the preceding century. His known paintings are workmanlike, but bubble with a curious life (*Ill. 139*). Like Decamps he ceaselessly sought new subjects, rare

139   JULES ROBERT AUGUSTE (*c.* 1789–1850)   *Study of Arab Horses*

and lustrous paint surfaces, and—again like Decamps—was one of those Romantics for whom the laboratory was almost as important as the studio. And he did have the merit of discovering Théodore Géricault (1791–1824) and of taking Géricault's advice to give up sculpture for painting. He also spread a taste for Orientalism by lending his friends the magnificent costumes which he had brought back from his visits to Africa.

In the nineteenth century Orientalism was not the passing and superficial fashion that it had been in the eighteenth, when Asia furnished picturesque curios and amusing oddities for Boucher's *chinoiseries*. In the nineteenth century artists were conquered by Morocco, Algeria and even the Moorish element in Spain. This was

149

not only in the realm of form and colour: the very spirit of the time was transformed deeply and for psychological as much as for plastic reasons. One could say that Orientalism played as large a part as the Gothic in the formation of Romanticism, and for the same reason: a need to escape from prosaic and banal reality into another world— it mattered little whether it was distant in space or time—which they believed to be freer, more beautiful and more stimulating.

Among the painters who set up their easels on the other side of the Mediterranean or beyond the Golden Horn, notable were Alexandre Gabriel Decamps (1803–60), Alfred Dehodencq (1822–82), Eugène Fromentin (1820–76), Marilhat (1811–47), Dauzats (1804–68) and Tournemine (1812–72). They are the best known of the explorer-artists, the pilgrims to the sun who were enchanted equally by the market-place and the desert, by African life and the infinity of open space which imposed no limits on contemplation or meditation.

Decamps, who in 1832 painted the moving *Defeat of the Cimbri*, one of the most beautiful works of French Romanticism, was to fulfil himself by painting amusing episodes from a Turkey that he had scarcely glimpsed, yet which continually fed his dreams and his art. This work places him among the best historical painters of his time, although his contemporaries blindly preferred the work in this genre of Paul Delaroche (1797–1856), Ary Scheffer (1795–1858), Eugène Devéria (1805–65) and F. J. Heim (1787–1865).

140   LOUIS BOULANGER
(1808–67)
The Phantoms   1829

141   LOUIS BOULANGER   *Sire de Gyac*

Sigalon (1787–1837), who painted *Athaliah Butchering the Royal Children* (1827, Musée des Beaux-Arts, Nantes), could have been another of the best Romantic historical painters if his life had not always thwarted the ambitions and paralysed the efforts of this poor and unlucky artist. At the Salon de Paris his *Athaliah* was very successful in 1827 but it was his only success. At the same Salon Delaroche showed his *Death of Elizabeth*, which was hailed as a work of genius, while Delacroix's *Death of Sardanapalus* went completely unnoticed. But a young painter, then only twenty-one, named Louis Boulanger (1808–67) revealed a fiery talent in a powerfully original painting called *Mazeppa* (now in the Musée de Rouen).

Boulanger chose to paint one of the static moments in a frightening story: the rebel being tied to a horse under the implacable and hate-filled eyes of his adversaries. While Boulanger may seem typical of

151

142 THÉODORE GÉRICAULT (1791–1824) *Raft of the 'Medusa'* 1819

Romantic dishevelment (*Ills. 140, 141*)—the equivalent of Petrus Borel the Lycanthrope, Napol the Pyrenean and Aloysius Bertrand in poetry and the novel—in such works as *The Hell Hunt* (1835), *Sabbath in a Church* (1828, a famous lithograph and perfect illustration for the 'horror novels' which England had brought into fashion), and *Scene of an Orgy* (1866, Musée de Dijon), which was inspired by his friend Victor Hugo, his *Mazeppa* shows contained violence, coiled upon itself and ready to explode.

When Géricault's *Raft of the 'Medusa'* (*Ill. 142*) was shown at the Salon in 1819, art-lovers were little prepared for an understanding of all that was implied by this pioneering and audacious work. Michelet, who did have some idea what it was about, wrote: 'It is France herself, it is all our society which is embarked on the raft of the Medusa.' Michelet also found the perfect epithet for this painter of madmen, the decapitated and the shipwrecked: 'the Correggio of suffering'.

3   THÉODORE GÉRICAULT   *The Madwoman*   *c.* 1822

The magic steed of the Romantics, the mount of the medieval paladins, of the Valkyries and of the accursed huntsmen, appears more
often in the work of Géricault than that of any other painter (*Ill. 145*).
It is an insistent, almost obsessive theme. His famous portraits of
Hussar and Dragoon officers, his *Artillery Attack* (*c.* 1814, Munich)
or his *Death of Hippolytus* (*c.* 1815, Musée de Montpelier) are only
occasions for expressing the great rebelliousness of these noble
animals, strange and secretive. Géricault was fascinated by the horse;
it was a subject where he found that movement from objective and
experimental reality to the Surrealist imagination which transfigures
and deifies a living being.

An analogous transposition is found in his portraits of madmen,
criminals and victims of the guillotine, revealing his imagination to
be oddly attracted to scenes of horror, madness and cruelty (*Ills. 143,
144*)—not through a diabolical lack of feeling, as was the case with
Goya, but for the value of such scenes as unique documentation, for
their monstrous strangeness, for their anomalousness. This man's
taste, described by Delacroix as 'extreme in all things', for hideous
sights and sinister enigmas of the human conscience, corresponds to
the important teratological side of Romanticism.

His paintings of a severed head beginning to decompose (Musée
de Genève), a man being tortured (1818, Art Institute of Chicago),
two severed heads (1818, National Museum, Stockholm) or of a
lunatic who believes he is a great general (1822–3, Oscar Reinhart's
collection, Winterthur) all have the same character as Rembrandt's
Flayed Ox (Louvre): Realism raised to the level of visionary
imagination, truth re-created by fancy, mundane exactness carried
to a monstrous and paradoxical splendour. This is one of the major
ambitions of Romanticism, which is realized in Géricault's sombre
and flashing genius.

The best proof of the numerous meanings which the word
Romanticism can convey is the difference between its 'traditionalist
wing' and that of Boulanger, Géricault and Delacroix. There we
find a painter whom it would appear more correct to call Classical:
Théodore Chassériau (1819–56). Certainly Chassériau found more
difficulty than most in detaching himself from the imprint and

144   THÉODORE GÉRICAULT   *The Murder of Fualdès*

constraint of Classical theory. Ingres had predicted, on seeing one of Chassériau's sketches executed when he was only twelve, that he would be 'the Napoleon of painting'. In fact the disciple cut himself away from his master's teaching when he reached maturity, but without graduating to a higher school; during his short life—he died when he was thirty-seven—Chassériau remained isolated and untouched by outside influences (*Ill. 146*).

Although the presence of some of Constable's paintings at the Salon de Paris in 1824 had been instructive, and the consequences of this lesson decisive, Romantic landscape painting in France does not date from then. We must go back to Watteau, Fragonard and Moreau the younger, even to Hubert Robert, to discover the origins of the pictorial revolution which affected not only their manner of

155

145 THÉODORE GÉRICAULT *Horse Frightened by Thunder and Lightning* 1820–21

seeing and representing nature, but even more the new concept of man's position in the universe and his connection with objects and the elements. For Watteau and Fragonard, landscape is no longer either objective or decorative: it becomes a state of mind, on the same grounds and almost in the same manner as poetry or music. The Romantic landscapists were more veracious, in the literal sense of the word, than Watteau and Fragonard, inclined to paint what they felt at least as much as what they saw, and striving to stay close to the 'facts'. They left the studio to paint nature as it actually is; they freed themselves from the restrictions of their predecessors and evolved a new aesthetic and an increasingly rich and supple technique. From that point begins the great wave which in the last years of the century leads to the Impressionists, to Cézanne,

156

146   THÉODORE CHASSÉRIAU (1819–56)   *Cossack Girl Finding the Body of Mazeppa*   1851

147   PAUL HUET (1803-69)   *The Beach at Villiers*

Van Gogh and Gauguin, where one can still find traces of that Romanticism which was the source of a new concept of nature.

Georges Michel (1763-1843) and Paul Huet, 1803-69 (*Ill. 147*) are the first definitely Romantic landscapists. They found in painters of the Dutch school such as Everdingen, Ruysdael, Seghers and especially Rembrandt, the models for a dramatic interpretation of nature. They steeped themselves in Shakespeare and were familiar with the tragic landscapes of *Macbeth* and *King Lear*, which they attempted to re-create wherever they found vistas which could be filled with tragedy by the play of light, or by a storm, or by the swift passage of clouds. There is something Shakespearian about *Sun Setting behind an Old Abbey* which Huet showed at the Salon in 1831, as there is in Friedrich's *Ruins of Eldena under Snow*.

These painters' choice of scenes indicates their predilection for those places which could be readily identified with an emotion of

158

the artist's: desolate marshes, deserted beaches, storm-tossed seas, thunder-clouds, sombre forests and bare rocks. Théodore Rousseau (1812–67) defined thus the common ideal of the first Romantic landscapists: 'Our art can only attain pathos through sincerity.'

This dramatic urge was so incomprehensible to the critics of the time that Rousseau's *Descent of Cattle from Pasture* (1835, Mesdag Museum, The Hague) was nicknamed by one of them *Descent of Cattle into Hell*. The sensitive and grandiose sobriety displayed by Rousseau, his talent for locating a place or a moment of the day in time and space (*Ill. 149*), were powerfully individual and filled with the expression of his emotional character. His *Gorges of Aspremont at Noon* (1857) forced him to paint increasingly on the spot and not to work from sketches in the studio. Rousseau loved the forest of Fontainebleau and the various untamed effects it offered, and came to settle in the near-by village of Barbizon. There he was joined by

148 ANTOINE CHINTREUIL (1816–73) *Space* 1869

149   THÉODORE PIERRE ETIENNE ROUSSEAU (1812–67)   *Sunset at Arbonne*

150   (opposite, above) CHARLES FRANÇOIS DAUBIGNY (1817–78)   *Evening*

151   (opposite, below) JEAN DÉSIRÉ GUSTAVE COURBET (1819–77)
The Roebuck in the Forest   1867

some of his friends, Romantic landscapists such as Charles Daubigny, 1817–78 (*Ill. 150*) and Diaz de la Peña (1807–76), who came to be known collectively as the Barbizon School.

Rousseau was certainly, as Focillon put it, 'the noblest soul and the greatest genius of the group'. However, long before the word was recast to describe the Impressionists, 'impressions' were appearing in Daubigny's paintings bathed in a transparent, silvery light where every drop of moisture glistens and shines. 'Impressions' were also recorded in the vast skies painted by Jules Dupré (1811–89), who revealed in his *Around Southampton* (1835) the spirit of Constable and the genius of the young Turner, and in the warm and sparkling texture of the Lyonnais Auguste Ravier (1814–95) as well as the bright and mellow greens of Antoine Chintreuil, 1816–73 (*Ill. 148*).

152 JEAN DÉSIRÉ GUSTAVE COURBET
The Sleepwalker 1865

These impressions are strongly personal and original means of feeling and expressing nature, not with a cold and scholarly objectivity, but with the sum of the infinitely rich and substantial exchanges which are established, in the act of artistic creation, between the thing seen, the soul of the artist and the thing created.

Although we can consider Gustave Courbet (1819–77) as a Realist and a Naturalist, because he shows people and things as they are without any idealization (*Ill. 152*), in fact an intense Romantic subjectivity exists in his work. The presence of the painter can be sensed in his least important sketch, even when he makes an objective reproduction of a rocky cliff towering above a river, or a tree-shaded pool where deer are drinking (*Ill. 151*), because the image is formed by his perception of it. He alone can express the *living experience* of nature, this state of intimate communion which is neither forced nor literary, as a pure effusion of his sensibility and a total comprehension of the momentary union of individual and object.

How many of his contemporaries understood the message of this artist, who in his *Dame de Francfort* (1858, Zürich Museum) expresses the Romantic melancholy as no other could, harmonizing the nostalgic sadness of the landscape with the morose figure of the

153 JEAN FRANÇOIS MILLET
(1814–75)
The Quarriers 1847–49

154 JEAN FRANÇOIS MILLET
The Wild Geese

155 HONORÉ DAUMIER
(1808–79)
Don Quixote and Sancho Panza
1865

woman whose desperate soul reflects the agony of the twilight?
None of those, surely, who condemned him as being no more than a
craftsman, and accused him of being a 'Realist through ignorance'
or even of 'laughing at himself, at others and at his art'. The Germans
understood him better, recognizing him after the 1876 exhibition at
Munich as the master of Romantic Realism. Later he influenced the
Realism of the post-Romantics Haider, Trübner and Leibl.

This same Romantic Realism, which we can also qualify as Social
Realism, reappears in the work of Jean François Millet (1814–75).
He shared his admiration between objective nature and Poussin.
This humble interpreter of work in the fields and the forests wished
to elevate episodes from country life to a style comparable to that of
the painter of *The Funeral of Phocion*. Even if the sentimentality of the
too-familiar *Angelus* (1857–9, Louvre) alienates us from him, one
must remember that no one has equalled him in experiencing and

156   JEAN BAPTISTE CAMILLE COROT (1796–1875)   *The Letter*

transmitting the experience of the smell of a woodcutter's fire on the verge of a forest in an autumn twilight, of paths and moisture-laden trees. These are the 'Georgics' of the Cotentin, filled with a poetry which does not recognize itself because it deals with the poetry of things in their impoverished and quotidian reality. But the secret of his art is to be found beyond this outward veracity, in its hidden inwardness, in its intimate and reserved yet passionate vibrations (*Ills. 153, 154*).

Here, too, is found the secret of Honoré Daumier's art (*Ills. 155, 157*). There are few figures more essentially Romantic than Don Quixote: one can easily understand how he so often inspired that bitter despiser of human mediocrity, a pessimist devoured by melancholy, a misanthrope attuned to the hidden life of things. But in the brown, russet and golden texture of his paintings, where a rare burst of colour sings with amazing life, and whose near monochrome serves him to express all the nuances and modulations of his feelings, there appears an indifference to any kind of lyric accentuation or chromatic orchestration.

157 HONORÉ DAUMIER *Rue Transnonain on April 15, 1834*

158　JEAN BAPTISTE CAMILLE COROT　*A Monk*

In the Ny Carlsberg Glyptotek at Copenhagen there hangs a strange painting by Camille Corot (1796–1875) entitled *Melancholy*. This painting, whose subject, like the enigmatic woman in Dürer's engraving, lets her eyes lose themselves in the unplumbed depths of exterior and interior abysses, probably dates from 1855. That is about ten years before *Interrupted Reading* (Art Institute of Chicago), which is treated in the same spirit. It prompts one to question the nature of Corot's Romanticism. When we consider these female figures we detect a Corot less familiar and less immediately accessible than Corot the landscapist, and intelligible only if we place him in the Romantic context (*Ills. 156, 158*). The figures are silent, vacant, foreign to their surroundings, isolated in an area with which they seem to have no communication, emptied of passion, waiting, perhaps vainly and yet eternally, for something which will fill up their vacancy of feeling and spirit.

159 GUSTAVE DO
(1832–83)
The Wandering Je
Crossing a Cemete

A sense of the fantastic plays a leading role in Romantic painting
as it does in literature, and was magnificently interpreted by both
painters and engravers. Gustave Doré (1832–83), who is best known
for his illustrations of Shakespeare, Dante, Cervantes and Rabelais,
was also a talented painter (*Ill. 159*). His *Ship Trapped by Icebergs*
(Musée de Strasbourg) was inspired by Wagner's *Flying Dutchman*
and by Caspar David Friedrich's *Wreck of the 'Hope'*. Doré was a

60 RODOLPHE BRESDIN (1825–85) *The Good Samaritan*

true visionary who put his excellent skill as a painter and engraver to the service of an inexhaustible imagination. Rodolphe Bresdin, 1825–85 (*Ill. 160*) was another visionary, whose engravings evoke nightmare scenes in extraordinarily luxuriant landscapes. He is familiar with the abysses which are bordered by despair and haunted by a tragic feeling which (as in the drawings and engravings by the sixteenth-century Swiss engravers) transforms the branches of dead trees into spectral forms and shows demon faces grinning from the folds of their bark.

Charles Meryon (1821–68), who died insane at the age of forty-seven, was a virtuoso of the interplay of black and white to which engraving lends itself best (*Ill. 161*). His vigorous accentuation of light and shade enabled him to express his sense of the mysterious presences which prowl around the great buildings of Paris, describing them with the precision of an architect and the scrupulousness of an archaeologist. He depicts dragons flying around the spires of Notre Dame and worms crawling along the walls of the streets. With Doré and Meryon we must rank Grandville (1803–47), an ancestor of the Surrealists and a master of the strange and bizarre. He was devoted to the quest of the 'marvellous' and the unusual, and he was an ingenious inventor of monsters. He multiplied their deformities, metamorphosed men into beasts and vice versa, and animated the most innocent objects with the same diabolical fierceness and energy which fills the canvases of Hieronymus Bosch.

The Romantic engravers revived and renewed all techniques, giving preference to the woodcut, and added to the rich potentialities of copperplate and wood the recent invention, by the German Alois Senefelder, of the lithographic stone. This was discovered about the beginning of the century and the vogue for newspapers and illustrated books provided it with a wide sphere of action. The Romantic period teemed with talented illustrators. Celestin Nanteuil's 'cathedral' frontispieces rank among the most interesting and characteristic works of the time. Edouard May, Camille Rogier, Jean Gigoux, the brothers Tony and Alfred Johannot, Achille and Eugène Devéria and, at a later date, Bertall perhaps give a truer and more complete idea of Romanticism—probably because engraving

161 CHARLES MERYON (1821–68)
The Ghoul 1853

underlines and exaggerates any peculiarities—than you can get from painting. Finally, what painter could give to the Rhenish burgs so dear to the Romantic imagination such a fantastic atmosphere as did Victor Hugo? He drew with whatever he found to hand: a cigar dipped in the dregs of his coffee was enough to conjure up devilish faces, medieval towns bathed in moonlight or dream landscapes buried in thick shadows.

'Let the trivial serve to express the sublime', said Millet. By this he meant transcribing everyday truth with a new dimension: that of the artist's interior world, which always seems suspect to strict Realists and even more to the Naturalists. Applying to painting the lesson given in literature by Emile Zola and the Médan school, they sought to identify and express the 'slice of life' only. This would hardly have suited Courbet, who claimed that one must 'create a living art by translating one's time' on to canvas. But there are various methods of 'translation'. The painter of the *Interment at Ornans*, while refusing to idealize, passes beyond material reality to render it sublime.

Throughout the history of French painting there runs a realistic tradition which emerged in the seventeenth century in the Le Nain brothers. But in the nineteenth century it meant something else to artists who had seen three revolutions—in 1789, 1830 and 1848—while awaiting the arrival of the Third Republic in 1871. Whether they wished it or not, political and social considerations intervened in their aesthetic; although Courbet, in his famous manifesto of 1855, had affirmed that the 'title of Realist had been thrust' upon him. Realism is a point of view which transcends the ordinary realm of art: it knows that it is revolutionary and opposed to Romanticism

162   JEAN BASTIEN-LEPAGE (1848–84)   *The Potato Gatherers*   1878

163   CHARLES JACQUE (1813–94)   *The Sheep-fold*   1881

and to all the Classical traditions which are hindered by academicism.
The systematizing spirit of the Realists made them try to create a
new world. The coming to power of the proletariat demanded that
the people should be represented in painting just as they are, the
sweaty workman with calloused hands, the peasant in the stupefied
condition to which he is reduced by toil in the fields. This led Ignace
François Bonhomme (1809–81), among others, to describe factories,
forges and foundries with a striking note of truth. Bastien-Lepage
(1848–84) stripped the field worker of the poetry with which Millet
had illuminated him (*Ill. 162*), to show him as an animal brutalized by
excessively hard labour, as in *The Haymaker* (1878). Charles Jacque,
who in his own time won repute as a painter of animals, preserved
in his depiction of stables and byres (*Ill. 163*) a discreet and concealed
lyricism which brings him close to Millet's sensibility.
    If one tries to form a comprehensive view of French painting prior
to Impressionism, which begins (chronologically) with the first

173

164   ELIE DELAUNAY (1828–91)   *The Plague at Rome*   1869

Impressionist show at the Nadar Gallery, one sees extremely different trends rubbing shoulders with one another, many of which are openly eclectic. While the Orientalist tradition inherited from Romanticism was continued in the work of Henri Regnault (1843–71), one finds in the work of Puvis de Chavannes (1824–98), especially in his great murals, a poetic feeling which borders on a disincarnated rather than an idealized or spiritualized Realism, and a whiff of academicism which one sees again in the *Decadence of the Romans* of Thomas Couture (1815–79). But both Puvis' and Couture's portraits show the greatest force and brilliance.

Although Millet and Courbet had wished to protect Romanticism from the contamination of various schools and of academicism in general—that is, from a teaching which was too much orientated towards the past and which could not look resolutely at the naked truth—it was this very contamination that produced a hybrid art. We see this in Elie Delaunay's *The Plague at Rome*, 1869 (*Ill. 164*), which harks back to antiquity, or in the mastery of bourgeois banality of Henri Gervex's *Communion with the Trinity* (1877). Carolus-Duran (1837–1917) derives from Courbet, but he was soon absorbed by worldliness, traces of which appear, despite his very attractive style, in portraits such as *Lady with the Glove* (1869). The influence of the ancient schools is a bit too obvious in the work of Ribera, a painter who nonetheless was in his own way as vigorous and original as Théodule Ribot, 1824–91 (*Ill. 165*).

165 THÉODULE RIBOT (1824–91) *St Sebastian* 1865

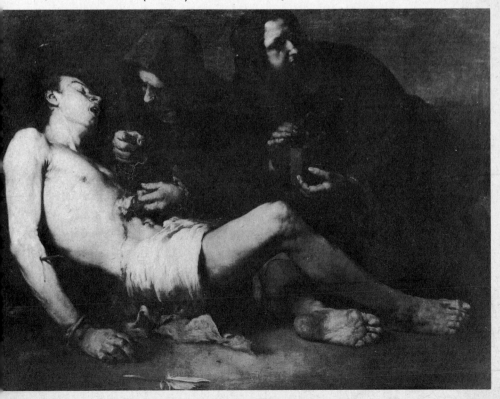

The best painters of the period between the end of Romanticism (which we may date from the death of Delacroix in 1863) and the first collective appearance of the Impressionists are those who are not constricted by any set style or formulae. Caillebotte (1848–94) was a forerunner of Impressionism and one of its most ardent defenders (*Ill. 166*); Frédéric Bazille (1841–70) was one of the most promising painters of his generation (*Ill. 167*), but unfortunately died in battle at the age of twenty-nine; Fantin-Latour (1836–1904) can be called the bridge between Romanticism and reality because of the nobility and dignity which he brings to his expression of truth—as, for example, in *Homage to Delacroix* (1864) and the *Studio at Batignolles* (1870). He exemplifies the wide gap between the lazy vulgarization of academicism and the hardihood of living art (*Ill. 168*).

166　GUSTAVE CAILLEBOTTE (1848–94)　*The Floor Planers*　1875

167 FRÉDÉRIC BAZILLE (1841–70) *The Family Reunion* 1867

168 HENRI FANTIN-LATOUR (1836–1904) *A Corner of the Table* 1872

Between 1860 and 1875 a radical change took place in the aesthetic of art, developing a new way of seeing forms and expressing them, along with a daring use of colour which led directly to the Impressionist technique. During this period of fifteen years the first Impressionist masters, Edgar Degas and Edouard Manet, joined the ranks of comparable geniuses among their contemporaries. They were of the same generation—one born in 1834, the other in 1832—and together they declared war on the conventions, sustained by the École des Beaux-Arts, which were loved by the general public and supported by official criticism. Manet's *Déjeuner sur l'Herbe* was painted in 1863, his *Olympia* (*Ill. 169*) in 1865, *The Fifer* in 1866, *The Balcony* in 1868. Degas painted *The Bellelli Family* (*Ill. 170*) in 1860 and *The New Orleans Cotton Exchange* in 1872. This was the opening of a splendid era, whose way had been paved by Romanticism, which reached its climax in Impressionism and was to last uninterruptedly until the great metamorphoses of form which distinguished the first years of the twentieth century.

169 EDOUARD MANET (1832–83) *Olympia* 1865

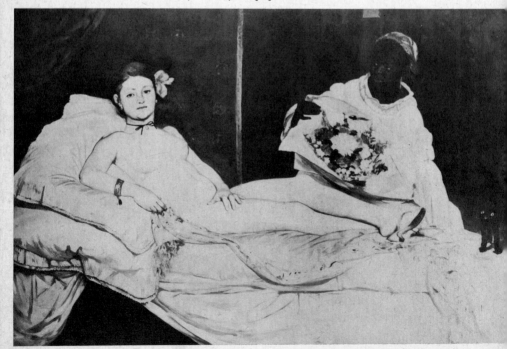

170   EDGAR DEGAS (1834–1917)   *The Bellelli Family*   1860

SPAIN

The majority of Francisco Goya's (1746–1828) biographers date his essential transformation from an artist in the eighteenth-century Rococo manner to a Romantic from the onset of the grave illness which attacked him in 1792. Perhaps he is *the* Romantic, for his sadly uneasy and passionate character was brought to the highest level of intensity. In 1792 he was forty-six and at the height of his fame; for twelve years Spanish society had recognized his genius as a portraitist and fought for the honour of sitting for him (*Ill. 171*). The court patronized him and named him official Court Painter in 1789. The

171 FRANCISCO GOYA (1746–1828) *Portrait of Dr Peral* c. 1795

172 FRANCISCO GOYA *The Young Girls* 1813

173 FRANCISCO GOYA
The Dream of Reason Produces Monsters
c. 1810–15

174 FRANCISCO GOYA
The Carnivorous Vulture
c. 1820

175 · FRANCISCO GOYA *Man Walking among Phantoms*

Madrid Tapestry Factory had commissioned the series in which he depicted the work and play of the Spanish people with the verve of Tiepolo and the rich colour of Fragonard. His work echoes with *joie de vivre*, with good-humoured malice and healthiness. His robust colours, sparkling with energy, marvellously portray the super-abundance of life which he possessed (*Ill. 172*).

'Always lines and never solid bodies. But where do we find lines in nature? I see only visible bodies and shapes which are not so, planes coming forward and planes which recede, reliefs and depressions.' Until 1792 his vision was suffused with radiance; both his being and his painting were bathed in sunlight. Although capable of aristocratic refinement, this Aragonese remained plebeian in the joyful and self-indulgent roughness with which he enjoyed life. His work has the elegant sensuality and hedonistic taste of the Rococo, but he was still the native of a grave and austere land. Working through instinct and passion, he seemed quite indifferent to the movements of ideas; he was all feeling, all vigour, but—with the

183

same blind vehemence which enabled him to find the absolute in a woman's body glistening with pearly lights—he was to tumble into a despairing pessimism, a total surrender to darkness and hell. His impulses were primitive and instinctive. This is probably why the illness which made him deaf brought about the change which made him embittered and inclined to see the ugliness and tragedy of life to the exclusion of any of its other aspects. In 1797 he rediscovered his old palette when he painted the cupola of Sant' Antonio in Madrid, where shapes form and disappear in a flash with a rustle of satin and pearls, although in the same year he engraved the *Caprichos*, a *danse macabre* in which this Tiepolo of the night summons from the shadows a disquieting band of monsters both ridiculous and deadly because they are human, and even too human.

But the fires of Goya's palette were progressively obscured and extinguished; murky blacks, poisonous greens, dull greys and livid whites began to produce their sharp dissonances. Like untuned instruments, his colours, although treated with an admirable and sure instinct for painting, clash with each other, tarnish one another and mingle their discordances. Not that he became negligent of his craft; on the contrary, it had never been more skilful than when its subjects were most repulsive. Goya was always eager to learn, and even taught himself lithography in 1819. He was sixty-nine, but the new technique, which he used in his *Tauromachia*, obtained for him a rapidity of execution, subtleties and shadows which he had never been able to realize in the woodcuts which he made of the nightmares of the *Disparates* (also called the *Proverbs*) engraved between 1816 and 1824, and the *Disasters of War* which were inspired by the terrible experiences of the French invasion, the Spanish resistance and the reprisals which followed.

If he was so willing to show warlike episodes in his paintings and engravings, it was in response to the attraction of the tragic, the hideous, anything which revealed imbecility, cruelty or the lucklessness of man to this pessimist, this prisoner of silence who retreated farther and farther into the darkness (*Ills. 173–5*). He spent most of his time in his country house, which he bought and decorated with frightful scenes as if his nightmares were not enough, as if he wanted

176 FRANCISCO GOYA *Saturn Devouring One of His Children* c. 1818

177   LEONARDO ALENZA (1807–45)   *The Romantics*

to be surrounded by such hallucinatory figures as Saturn devouring his children (*Ill. 176*), giants fighting in a morass, men flying, as one flies in a dream, towards the *nada* or nothingness, sorcerers seen laughing by lightning flashes while others brew criminal potions, and men perverted by the pleasure of infamous vices.

His paintings had such an influence over later Spanish artists that they prided themselves on seeing, thinking and painting like Goya,

178 EUGENIO LUCAS Y VILLAAMIL *The Prisoner* 1855

on coming as close to him as the unbridgeable gap between talent and genius permits.

The best quality of the rare Spanish Romantic painters such as Leonardo Alenza, 1807–45 (*Ill. 177*), Eugenio Lucas y Padilla (1824–70), Eugenio Lucas y Villaamil (*Ill. 178*) and José Parcerisa is their authentic and sometimes naïve imitation of Goya. Others, the Madrazos, followed lazily and without vigour or originality the

179 MARIANO FORTUNY (1838–74) *Marriage at Madrid* 1870

example of the French: the father imitating David, the son Delaroche. A whole generation of 'Davidians' appeared in Madrid, perpetuating a lifeless Classicism which killed the fruitful inheritance which Tiepolo bequeathed to Spain. Alenza deliberately caricatured Romanticism in his two versions of the Romantic suicide (the better is in the Romantic Museum in Madrid) which are like parodies of the 'horror novels'. He was sincere and led by Goya into frequenting hell, madness, sorcery and crime, which he recorded in dramatic woodcuts. In Goya, and Goya alone, Spanish Romanticism is born and reaches its climax. It has neither a yesterday nor a tomorrow, since the two Lucases, Alenza and Parcerisa are only extensions of Goya himself rather than truly original creators. Can one consider Solana's Expressionism, which is so strongly and deeply marked by

188

Goya's influence, as a form of post-Romanticism? It is a question which goes beyond the scope of this inquiry. For that matter, how would one discuss Dali's 'Goyaism'?

In any case, Spain, saturated by the tragic Naturalism which nourished its Romanticism, turned in the second half of the nineteenth century to a less dramatic notion of reality. At this moment, Mariano Fortuny (1838–74), a painter whose technique is skilful, brilliant and refined, produced pictures whose surface sparkles and gleams. The best of these, *Marriage at Madrid* (*Ill. 179*), hangs in Barcelona. It has been said, rather wittily, that Fortuny was 'a sketch by Goya imitated by Meissonier'. Certainly he was no more likely to start a great revival than was Daniel Urralieta Vierge, who is better known as an engraver and illustrator than as a painter.

Although Vierge is too literary and Fortuny too mannered, Joaquín Sorolla y Bastida (1863–1923), the painter of the fishermen and peasants of Valencia, may be classed among the true Realists. One appreciates his sincerity and vigour; and on the frontier where one perceives the beginnings of Impressionism (which in spirit correspond little to the grave, objective and almost severe character of the Spaniards) one must also recognize the Catalan Santiago Rusiñol (1861–1931), who was strongly influenced by his French contemporaries.

SWITZERLAND

Swiss painters were amazed to discover how fertile the mountains of their native land could be as a source of emotions, surprises and aesthetic joys. This was the period when Albert de Haller wrote his great poem on the Alps (which disturbed the Romantic sensibility as much as Young's *Night Thoughts* or Rousseau's *Reveries d'un Promeneur Solitaire*); when physicists, geologists and alpinists made the first ascents of the Alps for scientific rather than sporting reasons; when the Tyrolean Joseph Anton Koch became one of the first to realize the majestic beauty of untamed waterfalls and glaciers. The Swiss painters, in short, began to see that these landscapes were worth painting for themselves, and not simply as a background for some homely or dramatic scene.

'The most beautiful view leaves us unsatisfied if it is not animated by some foreground object which betokens the presence of our counterparts', wrote Charles-Albert Kasthofer. Liotard painted the little gardens of Geneva dominated by the bulk of the Salève, but only as an adjunct to his portrait of himself and also as a good excuse to show off his own garden. Although the Gabriel Lorys, father and son (1763–1840 and 1784–1846), and Johann Ludwig Aberli (1723–86) studied attentively and almost scientifically the nature of rocks, gushing waterfalls and torrential mountain streams, they always added an idyllic grace to their depiction of the wildest scenes, extinguishing the majesty and diminishing the austerity of the mountains. This is mingled with the kind of theism familiar to Rousseau; like Klopstock, they could detect in a waterfall a 'great thought of the Creator'. But their sensibility was not directly moved, and they were often inclined to slide into the bucolic.

The same true Romantic spirit is shown by J. J. Hürlimann (1793–1850) of Riedikon, by J. J. Biedermann (1763–1830) of Winterthur and by P. Birmann (1758–1844) of Basle, who was Aberli's best pupil. *Devil's Bridge* by Birmann, *Splügen Pass* by J. J. Meyer (1787–1858), and the *Gorges of la Douanne* by Dunker (1746–1807) are alive with the rustling of trees and the song of waterfalls; the strong wind of the mountain tops is more noticeable than the picturesque Alpenhorn, but these painters still lag behind the poets. Unlike Byron, none of them makes one feel that 'in these vaults of Ice, unalterably Sublime, dwells Eternity'. This privilege is reserved —and how parsimoniously distributed—to those Swiss artists for whom the mountains are an accomplished fact, where there are no more discoveries to be made: only ones to be tested and expressed.

Among the painters who preceded the true Swiss Romantics are Léopold Robert (1794–1835), although he preferred to paint truculent and theatrical brigands; the narrative painter Friedrich Rudolf Simon (1828–62); Jacques Laurent Agasse (1767–1849) who, like his compatriot Fuseli, was the darling of the English in his later years and who had a fine solid style, both vigorous and elegant, even though he is often called Romantic; Wolfgang Adam Toepffer (1766–1847), who gave in too easily to the sentimentality and comic

180 WOLFGANG ADAM
TOEPFFER
(1766–1847)
Girl with Bowed Head

banality of 'genre scenes' (*Ill. 180*); and Alfred van Muyden, who
was the prisoner of a rather mawkish temperament. A similar eclecticism marked the formation of Henry Fuseli (1741–1825), whose
thought developed equally from his reading of the old German epics
and Greek tragedy, with Shakespeare bridging the gap. His masters
in painting were Michelangelo and Rubens from the past, and, from
his own time, Reynolds. Fuseli was endowed with an imagination
which inclined towards the nocturnal aspects of life, and was
familiar with macabre apparitions and nightmares (*Ills. 181–3*). This

181 HENRY FUSELI (1741–1825)
Dante Meeting Ugolino
in the Frozen Cocytus c. 1774

182 (below) HENRY FUSELI
Odin Foreseeing
Balder's Death

183   HENRY FUSELI   *Lady Macbeth Grasping the Daggers*   c. 1801

led him to define his evolution almost like that of a sleepwalker in
the mists of the fantastic: 'I am crossing a sea which is shoreless and
unplumbed.' An authentic prophet, he made a lasting impression on
the work of Franz Pforr, Eberhard Wächter, Joseph Anton Koch
and Peter von Cornelius.

The great figures of Swiss Romantic landscape painting are Maximilien de Meuron of Neuchâtel (1785–1868), who set up his easel
on the shores of high mountain lakes, and scribbled in his sketchbook
in the middle of avalanches, and the sincere, vigorous François
Diday (1802–77). Thirty or forty years separate Diday's *Cascade de*

184 ALBERT DE MEURON (1823–97) *Chamois Huntsmen Resting* 1855

Pissevache, 1852 (*Ill. 186*) from that of Gabriel Lory the younger, but during those decades prodigious changes took place in the techniques and aesthetics, both authentically Helvetian, of modern painting. Gabriel Lory was simple and clumsy, because his subject intimidated him and because his intelligence failed to master the emotions aroused by the mountains; in Diday, on the other hand, whose *Mont Blanc Seen from Sallanches* (*Ill. 185*) swells with the grandeur of a symphony, one finds a harmony through which the artist becomes one with nature. This harmony was too often lacking in the painters of the preceding generation; they were never completely at home with the nature about them. But it is found in the paintings of Barthélémy Menn (1815–93), who must be considered a post-Romantic rather than a true Romantic. His supple and musical painting considerably influenced Ferdinand Hodler (1853–1918).

185   FRANÇOIS DIDAY (1802–77)   *Mont Blanc seen from Sallanches*

186   FRANÇOIS DIDAY   *Cascade de Pissevache*   1852

187   ALEXANDRE CALAME (1810–64)   *Landscape with Two Figures*

The greatest of this generation, which held such an intense communion with nature, was Alexandre Calame (1810–64). He profited
from the lessons of Italy, which he greatly loved, but without turning
from his proper interests. Calame was eclectic in taste, he preferred
to work in the open air, and he was intimately attuned to all aspects
of nature in those cantons which he wandered through, but he
retained enough of the idyllic tradition of the preceding century to
permit himself to depict a homely Switzerland at once rustic and well
looked-after (*Ills. 187, 188*). But Calame's true personality does not
appear in the tender scenes nor in the carefree pleasures of living in
well-kept spots. It is the tragic aspect of the mountains which appeals
first to him; he summons the outbreak of 'storms which he has willed'

188   ALEXANDRE CALAME
Mountain Landscape

(a goal of all the Romantics), and his world is that of forests bowed by the storm, streams leaping from their beds, heavy storm-clouds through which grey glaciers shine with the dull gleam of lead.

Calame's Romanticism stays within the bounds of Realism, but this very Realism is saturated with the supernatural and a unique and unusual quality of fantasy; we need no cloven hoof to realize that his *Summer on the Plain* (1850, Musée de Genève) is peopled with gods. That Swiss honesty (or perhaps a desire to remain within the bounds of the familiar) holds Calame back at the moment when these Pan-like forces would split the rocks or strip the bark from the trees—as does the nobility of his art, which keeps its restraint in the most dramatic moments.

The objective character typical of the body of Swiss painting has a particular significance in the work of the Bernese artist Ferdinand Hodler. If we look at his great murals on historical subjects, we see a robust and frankly stated veracity which enlarges his civic and military pomp, but in his allegories and landscapes the influence of Symbolism meets and fights with that of Realism. Nothing is more foreign to Naturalism than an interior life explained through allegories, even if the figures themselves are realistic. His motto was 'Eye, Intelligence, Heart'. The great metaphysical uncertainty of being and of becoming is always in the background of his pictures, even his landscapes, where the immediate representation of nature is infused with a feeling of panic comparable to that which inspired another great mountain painter, Giovanni Segantini. Among the high peaks of the Engadine, Segantini perceived in the spectacle of everyday reality the very pulse-beat of the cosmos.

SCANDINAVIA

The name of Asmus Jacob Carstens (1754–98) is often linked with Blake, Fuseli and Flaxman, and with good reason: the importance of this Danish painter, who had a greater influence on German Romanticism than he had in Scandinavia, stems principally from the great synthesis which he realized of the two great irreconcilables, Classicism and Romanticism. The originality of Carstens, who died at forty-four, lies mainly in his rejection of colour (*Ill. 189*). This rejection may be explained by the fact that his drawings are merely sketches for unfinished projects, or it may be that he considered— which seems far more likely—that a great artist can 'colour' as well as outline in black and white.

Although he had never seen the Sistine Chapel (since he had run out of money on his first visit to Italy in 1783, without getting any farther than Mantua), he knew and understood Michelangelo's genius better than did any of his contemporaries. He had seen nothing more than the work of Giulio Romano at the Palazzo del Té, but he discovered in Romano's frescoes, though they were far from his own ideal, the path which he should follow. It was not until 1792, when the generosity of a patron permitted him to return

189   ASMUS JACOB CARSTENS (1754–98)   *Night and Her Children Sleep and Death*

to Italy, that he reached Rome, where he was determined to end his days. However, he did not break with Scandinavian tradition; instead he wrote mythological plays with Wotan and Balder as heroes, Skaldic poems and imitations of *Ossian*.

Carstens' robust and generous individuality did not find any heirs in the Scandinavian countries; rather, it was Germany which inherited from him. There was, however, one field in which Carstens had followers: among painters who continued to find their inspiration in the old Nordic literature. Long after the fashion for Ossian and Wotan had disappeared in England and France—and

199

190 NILS JOHAN OLSSON BLOMMER (1816–53) *Water Sprite and the Daughters of Agir* 1850

even in Germany, where this was a native mythology—the sagas and ancient religious writings preserved their effectiveness in Denmark, and even more so in Norway, where the countryside is still peopled with trolls and giants.

The Swedish sculptor Bengt Erland Fogelberg (1786–1854) made several studies of the solemn and terrible face of Wotan. Among painters, Nils Johan Olsson Blommer (1816–53) depicted the gods of the Edda and the favourite heroes of the Skalds in both an idyllic and a tragic manner, but one realizes that for him this mythology no longer lived as it did for Carstens and Runge. It became formal 'historical painting', although a work like *Water Sprite and the Daughters*

191 NICOLAI ABRAHAM ABILGAARD (1743–1809) *Fingal's Ancestors Appearing to Him by Moonlight*

of Agir, 1850 (*Ill. 190*) shows a genuine talent which deserves to be better known outside the borders of Sweden. This also applies to the Danish artist Nicolai Abraham Abilgaard (1743–1809), who painted the great historical scenes in Christiansborg Castle which were destroyed by fire. He was trained in Italy and followed the example of the Venetians, whose colour he tried to apply to Northern settings, and Michelangelo. Obsessed by antiquity, he dreamed, like Carstens, of joining the Classical ideal of beauty to the sombre and ethereal power of Nordic mythology (*Ill. 191*).

Jörgen Valentin Sonne (1801–90) was another eclectic who studied in the Italian and Bavarian academies before settling in his

192   THOMAS BRUUN (1742–1800)   *Grotto*

native Denmark. He painted battles, compositions drawn from contemporary events, such as the revolt of the Tyrol against Napoleon and the Schleswig-Holstein War. He also painted religious scenes, thus leading people to say that he was at the source of a renewal of religious art, although an art, we must admit, which had neither much force nor much originality. He had been the best pupil of Christoffer Wilhelm Eckersberg (1793–1853), who is rightly considered as the father of modern Danish painting, more so in fact than the great Carstens.

One could write an entire book on the subject of the influence of Romanticism on theatrical décor. Here one would find that in

Germany Blechen was led to true Romanticism through having painted scenery for 'Sturm und Drang' plays under Schinkel's direction, and that Schinkel himself, before covering Berlin with those pseudo-Greek temples which justify his popular renown as an architect, had lavished on his scenery and his painting the passion he had for Gothic hugeness. In France another theatrical designer, Ciceri, left his immediately recognizable imprint on the majority of designers, such as the Johannots, Nanteuil and the Devérias, and quite a few painters who recognized the Gothic above all in the opera or melodrama.

193   PETER CRAMER (1726–82)   *The Death of Balder*

194 AUGUST FREDERIK AHLGRENSSON (1838–1902) *Grotto*

In Denmark there were at least five set-designers whose designs (preserved in the National Art Gallery in Copenhagen) show perhaps the closest connection of this country to European Romanticism. Two of them, Thomas Bruun, 1742–1800 (*Ill. 192*) and Peter Cramer (1726–82), designed sets both tragic and mysterious for one of the most dramatic episodes of the Edda: the death of Balder, the White God, slain through the treachery of the Fire God (*Ill. 193*). The grottoes painted by August Frederik Ahlgrensson (1838–1902) have an outlandishness and sombre secretiveness which is related to the mysteries of Scandinavian mythology (*Ill. 194*). Svend Valdemar Gyllich (1837–95) transposed into painting all the fire and brilliance of Wagner's orchestration in his décors for *The Valkyries* (*Ill. 195*). Jens Petersen Lund (*Ill. 196*) hovers on the borderline between the Rococo and Romanticism. He belongs to the eighteenth century in time only, and one hears in his work an echo of the great Italian

195   SVEND VALDEMAR GYLLICH (1837–95)   *The Valkyries*   1861

196   JENS PETERSEN LUND (1730–after 1793)   *Punch in Prison*

Baroque masters, Buornacini and Galli-Bibiena and of the French artist Servandoni.

Among portrait painters, there are few whom one would give the exact designation of Romanticism: they are rather Realists, some in the grand style and all robustly veracious. The only one who could be called Romantic is Jens Juel (1745–1802). A pupil of Abilgaard and later trained at Hamburg and Rome, he is famous for the finest portrait of the young Goethe. Juel's motto, which set him apart from the academic tyrannies, was: 'Paint only what you please, as you please.' This he did, and rightly, for his portraits are truly soulful, and his genre painting is full of graceful and light-hearted Realism.

Among Caspar David Friedrich's successors we can single out a young Norwegian who studied in Copenhagen before settling down in Dresden, Jens Christian Clausen Dahl (1788–1857). Memories of nature in his native land, of wild mountains, age-old forests, fjords tossed by the wind, glaciers sprawling in endless sheets of tortured

198   JENS CHRISTIAN CLAUSEN DAHL   *Landscape*   1826

white, roused a dramatic element in his feelings which are rare among the Scandinavian landscape painters of his time (*Ills. 197–8*).

Dahl was not satisfied merely to look at the landscape, he tested it in the recesses of his heart and was overpowered by the tragic presences which he could sense in it, which later haunted the landscapes of Edvard Munch. In this way he is a noble and remarkable exception from the bulk of Scandinavian landscape painting, which in general suffers from a sort of passive rusticity.

In this respect we must except the landscapes of the Swedish painter Elias Martin (1739–1818), although their lyricism is not always truly experienced. While retaining something of Rococo formalism, his landscapes are open to new passions. We must also except the work of his fellow countryman Per Hilleström (1732–1816), a likeable narrator of 'genre scenes' and conversation pieces, and who at least once achieved originality and grandeur in his *In the Foundry* (*Ill. 199*).

199 PER HILLESTRÖM (1732–1816) *In the Foundry* 1781

The most esteemed genre and domestic painters, such as Wilhelm
Marstrand (1810–73) and Constantin Hansen (1804–80), scarcely
figure in the history of Romantic painting; they are skilful and
lovable minor masters, anecdotists, from whom one expects ravish-
ing descriptions of the life of Danish painters in Rome or of the
amusing surprises of the streets of Copenhagen. Neither Rörbye
(1803–48), who studied in Eckersberg's school, nor Christian Köbke
(1810–48) is distinguished by a genuinely Romantic accent. Their
love for reality preserves a shade of touching naïvety which is worthy
of respect, but their paintings generally lack interior life; their landscapes are not inhabited by the gods—they are on man's scale,
designed for man's use and for his pleasures.

Peter Kristian Skovgaard (1817–75), Christen Daalsgaard (1824–1907) and Johann Thomas Lundbye (1818–48), who are all Danish, and the Swedes Johan Gustaf Sandberg (1782–1854) and Per Gabriel Wickenberg (1812–46), might almost be placed in the wake of the minor Dutch masters of the eighteenth century rather than among the Romantics of the nineteenth. The timidity too often brought by the Scandinavians to their acceptance of Romanticism and their manner of interpreting it is a constant source of surprise for the art historian, especially when we remember the close links which existed between the artistic centres of northern Germany and Copenhagen, and above all the supremacy of the Art School in that city where so many Germans came to study at a time when its only rival was Paris.

ITALY

It is undoubtedly inaccurate or at least insufficient to explain Italy's absence from the Romantic movement in painting by attributing it to the political circumstances which cost Italy her independence; especially since Romantic music was well represented in the peninsula, and her greatest nineteenth-century poets were definitely Romantics: Leopardi, Carducci and Foscolo. One must seek another reason why, after six centuries of an incomparable flowering of genius in the plastic arts, this triumph should end in near sterility at the very moment when Realism could have given it new brilliance.

Who were the Italian contemporaries of Delacroix, Friedrich and Constable? There were painters more or less directly descended from Pompeo Batoni or Mengs, such as Gasparè Landi (1756–1830) or Vincenzo Camuffini (1773–1844), both neo-Classicists. There were Andrea Appiani (1754–1844) and Giuseppe Borsi (1777–1815), and imitators of David such as Pietro Bienvenuti (1769–1844) and Francesco Hayez (1791–1882), who painted worthy portraits and who mastered a rather 'troubadour' style in genre paintings (*Ill. 200*) —half homely, half theatrical—such as Hayez's over-praised *Romeo and Juliet* (1859, Gallery of Modern Art, Milan). Although David's imitators preserved a French streak, there is another group which paradoxically was influenced by the German Nazarenes, and whose

200   FRANCESCO HAYEZ (1791–1882)
The Kiss   c. 1859

201 TOMMASO MINARDI (1787–1871) *Trojan Women Lamenting over the Body of Hector* 1823

aesthetic was governed by the discussions at the Monastery of San Isidoro and the frescoes of the Bartholdy Casino. The painters who sought inspiration at the Villa Massimi at the same time nurtured an ideal of medieval and almost monastic purity. They wished to renovate religious art according to Wackenroder's principles, revealed to them by Overbeck and Cornelius; and they set out, in the train of 'the monk in love with art', to rediscover medieval or, more accurately, Renaissance painting.

The painters grouped under the label of Purists had at their head Luigi Mussini (1813–88). Although he was the youngest of them, he was also the most talented. Maximilian Seitz (1811–88), an Italianized German, Antonio Marini (1788–1861) and Tommaso Minardi, 1787–1871 (*Ills. 201, 202*) deserve mention only because, almost alone in a tradition of original and daring personalities, they practised an imitative art, almost indeed an art of pastiche.

202   TOMMASO MINARDI   *Self-portrait*

The Verists are more interesting in every respect since they stayed within the fruitful main stream of the Italian genius: observation and faithful representation of reality. Their work marks a frank and almost hostile reaction to the Purists' idealism, which was strongly tainted with artificiality. Thanks to these periodical returns to reality, Italian art had perpetually renewed itself since the time of Giotto and Cavallini. Yet we find no more creative spirits among the Verists than among the Purists, though these supporters of the cause of reality at least steered painting into a less sterile path than that taken by the post-Nazarenes. The Realist aesthetic responds in other ways to tendencies which are more complex than pure Naturalism. There is still a strong 'literary' element in the work of Nicolò Barabino (1832–92), Francesco Netti (1834–94) and, the best of them, Domenico Morelli (1826–1901). They employed, in place of strict observation of everyday reality, a theatrical reality; they treated banal episodes with Romantic lyricism, and then treated historical, literary and theatrical subjects with an affected Naturalism. This arbitrary aesthetic, which could be related to that of Verdi and Puccini in music, is evident in Giacinto Gigante's *Festa della Madonna dell'Arco* (*c.* 1811, Naples Museum), *St Francis' Vision of the Cross* by Gabriele Smargiassi (private collection, Naples) and *The Death of Tasso* by Morelli (*Ill. 203*).

203 DOMENICO MORELLI (1826–1901) *The Death of Tasso* *c.* 1860

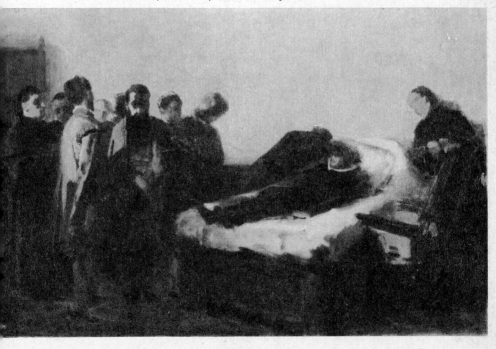

204 GIACINTO GIGANTE (1806–76) *Fountain of the Temple of Serapis, Pozzuoli* 1841

The austere simplicity of the Purists and the rather strident rhetoric of the Verists is perhaps more sentimental than Romantic. Yet at the same time as these diverse trends we notice Delacroix's mark on Morelli, especially in his *Daughter of Jairus*. Like the painter of *Women of Algiers*, Morelli had discovered the fascination of Africa, and thus started a new wave of Orientalism, which remained in fashion for a time.

After Mussimo d'Azeglio (1798–1866) showed the way, the taste of the Italian painters turned towards their own countryside, which had aroused the passion and the nostalgia of so many English, French, German and Scandinavian painters. The Neapolitan school, known

as the Posillipo school, which included Edoardo Dalbono (1841–
1915) and Filippo Palizzi (1818–99), set itself to depict with absolute
fidelity the features and spirit of the Italian landscape. These painters
were Romantic in the watchful tenderness they felt for nature
and in the poetic feeling which inspired the interpretation they
gave to it.

A few traces of Romanticism remain in the Macchiaioli (otherwise
known as the 'Tachistes') of the latter half of the nineteenth century,
among whom can be found many original and interesting minor
masters. Tranquillo Cremona, 1837–78 (*Ill. 205*), Giacomo Favretto
(1849–87), Paolo Michetti (1851–1929) and Telemaco Cremona
show its finest expression, which is both popular in spirit and literary
in inspiration, mingling the realism of the theatre with reality itself.
In their lifetime these artists enjoyed enormous success because they

205 TRANQUILLO CREMONA
(1837–78)
The Two Cousins 1870

supplied exactly what Italian society wanted at that time. They were as much liked by the bourgeoisie as by the common folk because they represented something of the aesthetic of the theatre, the opera and music, which were the trend-setters of popular taste. For this reason these artists should perhaps be considered in a history of taste rather than in a history of art, if it is possible to separate one from the other.

THE LOW COUNTRIES

Belgium contributed to European Realism several historical painters who harmonized the beautiful pictorial traditions of the Low Countries with a sincere lyricism and realism devoted to the objective truth of beings and objects, plus one painter of genius: the paradoxical, morbid and uneven Wiertz, who developed from social-naturalistic mawkishness to a visionary imaginativeness which was later echoed by James Ensor. Belgian Romanticism, spurred by the notions of liberty, independence and social progress which enlivened the generation of 1830, was proud to renew its ties with the former art of its country. 'Long live Belgium and long live Rubens' was the rallying cry of the painters who celebrated the finest hours of their national history while still painting in the old style without any desire for modernity or even originality. For these artists it was enough to proclaim their firm resolve to break with the ideas and forms of the eighteenth century, and to reaffirm a patriotism which political events roused to boiling-point in all classes of society in all civic activities.

Because they derived their authority from Rubens, the historical painters Louis Gallait (1810–87), Hendrik Leys (1815–69) and Gustave Wappers (1803–74) were faithful to a sound and clear aesthetic in the continuity of the 'beautiful masterpieces' of times past. *Leaving Mass* (*Ill. 206*) by Hendrik Leys, or *The Capture of Antiochus by the Crusaders* (*Ill. 207*) by Gallait are, like Wappers' *Episode from the Belgian Revolution* (Brussels), an act of homage to the Old Masters. However, one must not ignore the new feeling which appeared in them for the 'page of history' Romantically conceived and expressed.

206   HENDRIK LEYS (1815–69)   *Leaving Mass*   1866

Leys is closer to the German painters of the Düsseldorf school
than to the French whom Gallait rather over-admired, especially
Delaroche. He frequently discovered a modern feeling in the composition of his pictures and even more in his treatment of colour.
This painter, who died prematurely at the age of forty-four, showed
both the possibilities and the means of a renewal which he himself
unfortunately lacked time to accomplish. In the same way, Antoine
Wiertz's madness, the caprices of an extravagant imagination, often
misguided and exposed to ridicule the very real talent and the
impetuous originality of this marvellous solitary.

Wiertz brought the perfect technique to the service of his visionary fancy: precise and fastidious, it could as easily caress the pearly and Rubenesque flesh of *La Belle Rosine* (*Ill. 209*) as reveal in a flash with stunning pyrotechnics the world trodden by his *Giant*. In the *trompe-l'œil* of stalls at a fair, the melodramatic horrors of *Buried Alive* and *Woman Eating Her Child*, it was their photographic Naturalism that was Wiertz's pride. He was drunk with his powers of illusionism, but the sincerity and simplicity found in his paintings tempered his almost pathological megalomania. Wiertz's work is spoiled by a predilection for the horrible and the monstrous which he perversely cultivated; yet if one considers the troubled imagination which directed it and the fire with which his best pictures are

207 LOUIS GALLAIT (1810–87)
*The Capture of Antiochus
by the Crusaders* 1843

208 LOUIS GALLAIT *Two Children*

209 ANTOINE JOSEPH WIERTZ
(1806–65)
La Belle Rosine

painted, his work is not unworthy to hang beside the great Romantic 'eccentrics', those unique but incomplete geniuses who draw our curiosity and hold our sympathy.

One might say that Wiertz's Surrealistic Naturalism is actually Realism pushed to the extreme and even to the absurd. Yet we find Constantin Meunier, 1831–1905 (*Ill. 210*), whose sculpture we have already considered, moving in the direction of a more sober and objective art, inspired by social ideas derived from the French Revolution. We also see the 'Group for Free Art', which exercised a strong influence on Belgian painting. This movement, which sought reality in its pure state—an almost photographic reality—although it was tainted with a socialist idealism, found its origin in the repercussions among Belgian artists of the Courbet exhibition in 1851. As a result of this exhibition, Courbet's *Stone Breakers* became their symbol and rallying-point. Revolutionary traditions, always alive in

210   CONSTANTIN MEUNIER (1831–1905)   *Collieries under Snow*

Belgium, found in pictorial socialism the visual embodiment of political claims upheld by a powerful and unsubdued vitality. The echo of this trend survives into the twentieth century in the neo-Realist movement started by the Laethem Saint Martin group.

Belgian art also takes into consideration the tendency of religious art to impregnate peasant life with its spiritual values, a tendency which inspired Van Gogh during his missionary period in the Borinage. Van Gogh's desire to represent reality and the burden of daily life in an almost sacred atmosphere was anticipated by Charles de Groux (1825–70), whose *Benedicite* in the Ghent Museum shows the same collective piety expressed in those biblical scenes in modern dress by Fritz von Uhde, whose religious Naturalism was combined with symbolist tendencies, at roughly the same period as the German Worpswede Group.

211 FERDINAND DE BRAEKELEER (1792–1883) *The Count of Mi-Carême at Children's School*

Belgian Realism, however, is not only social Realism. In the work of Henri de Braekeleer (1840–88) it returned to the intimacy of the minor Dutch masters of the seventeenth century. He recalls a humourless Spitzweg, who had a taste for collecting and for antiques. Braekeleer took no subjects beyond his home and the streets of his quarter; he was faithful to the narrow universe that he loved and which belonged to him (*Ill. 212*). All its facets are depicted with a tactile feeling for its materials; Braekeleer was full of delicacy and

222

212 HENRI DE BRAEKELEER (1840–88)
Man at the Window

213 ALFRED STEVENS (1817–75)
Ophelia

214 JOHANNES BOSBOOM (1817–91) *Geertekerk Utrecht*

feeling, with a sensual preference for what he could caress with his hands. With the same tactile sensitivity with which Braekeleer obtained almost illusionist effects, Alfred Stevens (1817–75), known as 'the prodigal son of Romanticism', became the foremost painter of women of his time (*Ill. 213*). He lacked the *brio* and virtuosity of Boldini, but he had a very good feeling for truth. But this feeling was somewhat diluted by his gracefulness, which warrants his being called the Mieris or the Netscher of the eighteenth century. However, his compatriot Félicien Rops (1833–98), more an engraver and illustrator than a painter, revelled in a morbid and brutal eroticism, which tried to be Naturalist but rather achieved a Surrealism comparable to that of his forerunner Breughel the elder.

215 B. C. KOEKKOEK (1803–62) *Mountainous Landscape*

216 W. J. J. NUYEN (1813–39) *Landscape with Ruins* 1836

217 JOZEF ISRAËLS (1824–1911) *A Son of the Chosen People*

At all times one of the most characteristic elements of painters in the Low Countries is their faithfully objective representation of daily reality: in the still-lifes of the religious painting of the Renaissance, and even more in the portraits, landscapes (*Ills. 215, 216*), domestic scenes and *vanitas* of the seventeenth century. In the nineteenth century there appeared painters like J. Bosboom (1817–91), Saenredam's successor in paintings of the interiors of churches (*Ill. 214*), and Jacob Maris (1837–99), whose skill enables the spectator to feel, in his pictures of town and country, the weight of the earth and the depth of the water in the canals. These painters used new materials, but in a spirit which was very close to that of their predecessors and which gave a new vitality and nobility to that love of nature which has always stimulated Dutch art.

One finds this tender and almost timid passion for the object in the paintings of the reserved and enigmatic Jozef Israëls (1824–1911), whose works seem redolent, both to the smell and to the touch, with the sensual presence of simple things from the junkshop or the stall of the old-clothes merchant. In these paintings the sordid and mysterious poverty of the Jewish quarter, where Rembrandt had once lived and which he loved, embraces the Romanticism of humble things and people, an evocation of a life whose objectives are obscure—reproduced with the misty atmosphere of twilight and half-light (*Ill. 217*). Such qualities make one hesitate in assigning Israëls' work to either Romanticism or Realism.

RUSSIA

If one compares the pictorial Romanticism of Russia with the genius of her poets who were creating at that time the peak of Russian literature, one must deplore the absence of a Pushkin or a Lermontov to guarantee the renown of Russian painting throughout Europe. To explain the poverty of Russian Romanticism, especially in comparison with that of Germany, France and England, one must invoke not so much the absence of an aesthetic tradition as the tyranny of these traditions. Although religious art deliberately confined itself to the repetition of forms established several centuries before by the schools of Pskov, Moscow and Novgorod, in the Byzantine line,

218 CARL BRULLOV (1800–52) *Last Day of Pompeii* 1828

profane art followed the fashions of Paris and Berlin step by step and was cherished by the cosmopolitan high society which was proud to be de-Russianized. Popular art, which had sprung up in the country for the country people, was itself virtually immobile and repeated unchanging themes with the same means.

The genre painting of Alexis Venetsianov (1780–1847) and Paul Andrevitch Fedotov (1815–52) is skilful, theatrical, 'humorist' and documentary; but as art it never goes beyond the level of an extremely learned and prudent academicism. This is why we are touched by the ambitious *Great Machines* of Brullov. They possess something that the 'petty-bourgeois' or 'squirearchical' art of Venetsianov and Fedotov lacks: Brullov's aspiration to equal the Old Masters (*Ill. 219*). The particular masters whom Brullov wished to equal were Michelangelo and the Raphael of the 'Stanze'; ironically, however, his *Last Day of Pompeii* (*Ill. 218*) is both the best and at

219   CARL BRULLOV   *Design for a Fountain*

the same time the most revealing example of this aspiration, for it shows how far he lagged behind the Old Masters.

The reverse is true of Alexander Ivanov (1806–58). Turgenev clearly summed up the difference between these two personalities, who enjoyed an equal fame in their own country, when he said: 'Brullov had the gift of expressing whatever he wanted to, but he had nothing to say. Ivanov had plenty to say, but his tongue stuttered.' In Rome, Ivanov had frequented the Nazarene circle. He was particularly close to Overbeck, whom he greatly admired, and adopted the ideals and the aesthetic of that Guild ensconced in the Monastery of San Isidoro. He was enchanted by philosophy and in love with mysticism, and he tried to express all his religious thought in a painting showing Jesus appearing to the people on the bank of the River Jordan (*Ill. 220*). This task seemed so important to him that he judged himself both artistically and spiritually unready to express the feelings which possessed him. He literally consecrated his whole life to it, accumulating studies and sketches, and only his material circumstances prevented him from going to settle in Palestine in order to recapture the atmosphere and local colour which might have given some life to the painting. It was laboriously conceived and perpetually revised by his demanding will, which was never satisfied; as one might expect, the picture turned out to be laborious, cold, inert and incontestably noble, but bereft of the soul with which he meant to endow it.

Perhaps Ivanov would have shown his real stature if he had completed—or even attempted—the colossal decorative compositions, of which he dreamt, for a monumental Temple of Humanity. Here again his preparation was too long and too painstaking, leading him to study not only Palestinian but also Egyptian and Assyrian archaeology, thus paralysing the creative effort of this over-scrupulous painter. If he had lived twenty years longer, the Temple of Humanity might have become one of the most grandiose expressions of Slavic Romanticism, which in painting lacks its Gogol or its Tchaikovsky.

Tchernichevsky's *Essay on the Relation between the Beautiful and the Real*, which appeared in 1865, was the origin of a very important

220 ALEXANDER IVANOV (1806–58) *The Manifestation of Christ to the People*

aesthetic revolution dedicated to the demise of the Romantic tendency to idealize reality and substitute for it a preference for objective Naturalism—powerful, energetic and sometimes brutal, and which finds its supreme moment in the socialist Realism recognized and imposed as the State Art by Soviet Russia. Tchernichevsky's work supported a campaign which was being very actively pursued by the intelligentsia to give art the finality of an educational medium. In 1863, two years before the publication of the *Essay*, travelling exhibitions were organized. They toured all the towns and villages with art masterpieces in order to initiate into the cult of beauty the illiterate populace of the country and the equally unlettered working classes of the towns.

The refinements of technique and feeling characteristic of Romantic idealism no longer answered to the programme which they wished to carry out, and they had to offer the people an art which conformed to popular tastes and desires. This consisted of easily identified and slavish reproductions of everyday things down to the least detail. Pictorial Naturalism seemed to be trying to rival photography. The famous *Peasant and Bride* painted in 1883 by Ivan Kramskoy (1837–87) was important as a manifesto. In fact, Kramskoy had refused to compete for the Gold Medal when he was at the Art Academy because the subject was taken from Scandinavian mythology, and he became one of the most active promoters of the Association for Travelling Exhibitions, at the same time as Nicholas Gay (1831–94), who was inspired by the same ideals.

Gay had painted religious and historical subjects until his reading of Tolstoy converted him to his didactic mission and to the popular Realism which was one of the articles of faith of the travelling exhibitions. To teach the townspeople and the peasants, to introduce the ignorant *moudjik* to the beauty of art, was for Gay and Kramskoy

222   VASSILY VERESHCHAGIN (1842–1904)   *Apotheosis of War*   1871

a new rule for living. Gay's *Portrait of Alexander Herzen* (*Ill. 221*) shows his cautiousness in not adding anything to the almost photographically accurate representation of his sitter, as if an emotion capable of striking and arousing the masses could come only from this objective precision.

In Gay there is no trace of the ideology and symbolism which dictate Vassily Vereshchagin's famous canvas *Apotheosis of War*, 1871 (*Ill. 222*). This 'plea for peace' had been suggested to the painter by his personal experiences as a war correspondent in Turkestan. In this painting reality is transcribed with an almost brutal simplicity, and the lesson contained in the pyramid of severed heads does not need a commentary to get its message across to the spectator. Painting had moved from the Romantic symbolism of Brullov and Ivanov

233

223   ILYA REPIN (1844–1930)   *Bargemen of the Volga*   1872

to a 'speaking allegory' whose meaning even the most ignorant could grasp.

Because it was understood by people from all levels of society and of all degrees of culture, artistic creation in the latter half of the nineteenth century was conditioned into becoming utterly foreign to Fedotov's graces and refinements. He was the leader of the Naturalist school contemporary to Romanticism, but there was nothing 'Naturalist' about it apart from the name. Certainly in Fedotov's *Little Widow*, 1851 (*Ill. 224*) there is a quietly intense poetry

224   PAUL ANDREVITCH FEDOTOV (1815–52)   *Little Widow*   1851

225   ISAAK LEVITAN (1861–1900)   *Spring Waters*   1897

about the familiar objects with which the bereaved woman is surrounded.

At the age of thirty, Vassily Perov was in Paris on a scholarship at the École des Beaux-Arts and there found himself in contact with the French Realists. He knew and was greatly influenced by Gustave Courbet. He admired Meisonnier, whom he imitated even in his cold and painstaking descriptions of observable truth. But after his return to Russia he too was taken by the idea of the travelling exhibitions, and set himself in art to telling the life story of the Russian peasant. During this same period, the Russian peasant was also the inspiration for Ilya Repin's best-known pictures, *Bargemen of the Volga*, 1872 (*Ill. 223*) and those Realist 'slices of life' inspired by political events: *Return from Siberia*, *The Propagandist's Arrest*, or his very picturesque and vivid picture *The Zaporogean Cossacks Writing a Letter to the Turkish Sultan*, whose subject came from Gogol's *Taras Bulba*.

Repin may be considered as the artistic ancestor and model of present-day Soviet painters such as Grekov, Guerassimov and the Kurinskys. But he had a greater faculty for dominating his subject rather than being restrained by it as is too often the case today. As well, Repin had worked in France between 1873 and 1876, but avoided enrolment in the Naturalistic school through a sense of burning eclecticism which also prevented him from enlisting in the ranks of such a pinched and impoverished Naturalism as that of Soviet Realism. Like Isaak Levitan (1861–1900), who brought about a revolution in Russian landscape painting (*Ill. 225*), Repin abjured all systematic and doctrinaire approaches. His absolute and sincere devotion to reality was accompanied by a lyric feeling which gives his work a higher and wider effectiveness.

THE UNITED STATES

Two currents determined the course of Romanticism in America. The first, originating in Europe towards the end of the eighteenth century, reflected some of the Old World's moods of disillusion and revolt against the empty forms of Classicism; the second, emanating from more purely indigenous sources, was fed by the dream and optimism of the young, rapidly expanding nation. It was natural that the first stirrings of the Romantic temper in a people then largely of British stock should have come for the most part from the mother country. At the height of English neo-Classical painting in the last quarter of the eighteenth century there could be detected the seeds of Romanticism. Some of the manifestations of those characteristic Romantic emotions—passion, terror, mystery, horror—are found in the work of two American Realists with a distinctly native flavour: John Singleton Copley (1738–1815) and Benjamin West (1738–1820). Although West, who was born in Chester County, Pennsylvania, migrated to England where he developed the 'grand manner' and became the second president of the Royal Academy, he uninhibitedly turned from purely classical subjects for his historical paintings to the then novel themes of the Bible and English and American history, such as *Penn's Treaty with the Indians* (*c.* 1771, Pennsylvania Academy of the Fine Arts). It is also noteworthy that some of his middle and late work is strongly tinged with Romantic feeling, particularly in the eerie *Saul and the Witch of Endor* (1777, Wadsworth Atheneum, Hartford, Conn.) and *Death on the Pale*

226 BENJAMIN WEST (1738–1820) *Death on the Pale Horse* 1802

227   JOHN SINGLETON COPLEY (1738–1815)   *Watson and the Shark*   1778

Horse, 1802 (Philadelphia Museum of Art, *Ill. 226*), which anticipated by twenty-five years the drama and animation of Delacroix's *Death of Sardanapalus*. As for Copley, despite the uncompromising Realism of his early portraits, before he moved to England and adapted himself to the fashionable Rococo portraiture, there was also a Romantic strain in the ambitious historical paintings he executed shortly after his arrival in London. The first of these is *Watson and the Shark*, 1778 (*Ill. 227*), recording with powerful evocation of horror an actual event from contemporary life. Not until Géricault's *Raft of the 'Medusa'* (*Ill. 142*) forty years later was a painting to depict in such powerful terms man's struggle against nature.

Another American narrative painter, Jonathan Trumbull (1756–1843), son of a Connecticut lawyer and patriot, celebrated contemporary history in slightly different terms (*Ill. 228*). After serving briefly as aide-de-camp to Washington and a year of study in London with West, he turned to painting a series of compositions glorifying the American Revolution. For these he made incisive miniature portraits of the signers of the Declaration of Independence in preparation for the huge murals in the Rotunda of the Capitol in Washington. An admirer of Rubens, he painted with spirited action and luminous colour such compositions as *Sortie of the British Garrison from Gibraltar*, which has been characterized by the critic Edgar Richardson as 'worthy of the greatest Baroque narrative paintings.'

The first truly Romantic painter in America and certainly the most important American landscapist of the early nineteenth century was Washington Allston (1779–1843). Born on a rice plantation in South Carolina where—like Poe—he was deeply impressed by tales of witches and ghosts, he moved at an early age to Newport, R.I. During these formative years he was an inveterate reader of German and English Romantic literature, including Mrs Radcliffe's widely read *Mysteries of Udolpho*, which was published in America in 1795 and for which Allston did some illustrations. In 1801 he went to London, where he was received by Benjamin West and learned the colouristic techniques of underpainting and glazes stemming originally from Venetian painting, which were the key to Romantic painting. An ardent admirer of Fuseli and Salvator Rosa, he had little use for the English portrait painters. In 1803 he went to Paris with John Vanderlyn (1775–1852), and then to Rome, where he frequented the Caffè Greco, international haunt of Romantics such as Shelley, Keats, Thorwaldsen, Turner and James Fenimore Cooper. It was in Rome that Allston first met Washington Irving, whose tales of the Hudson River Valley and characters like Rip Van Winkle and Ichabod Crane were to bring him lasting fame. There he also formed a friendship with Samuel Taylor Coleridge, who became deeply interested in Allston's work. He was at this time painting a series of imaginative landscapes in a grandiose and dramatic mood (*Ill. 229*), notably the chaotic and tempestuous *Rising of a*

228   JONATHAN TRUMBULL (1756–1843)   *Declaration of Independence*   1786–97

Thunderstorm at Sea (1804, Museum of Fine Arts, Boston) and *The Deluge* (1804, Metropolitan Museum of Art, New York). In the latter he gave full play to his Romantic temperament in an eerie vision of nude figures washed up by huge waves on a lonely beach where serpents and a howling wolf appear on the scene. On his return to America, Allston's work became quieter, more lyrical and dreamlike in such canvases as the luminous *Moonlit Landscape* (1819, Museum of Fine Arts, Boston) and *The Flight of Florimel*, 1819 (Detroit Institute of Arts, *Ill. 230*), the latter a colourful figural composition based on an episode in Spenser. In these imaginatively narrative compositions, Allston brought American painting out of the narrow confines of the stiff colonial portraiture into a monumental style and

241

229 WASHINGTON ALLSTON (1779–1843) *Ships at Sea*

the use of ideal subject matter. According to Richardson, the luminosity and resonance of tone which he had learned from Venetian painting 'set new standards of subtlety and atmospheric richness. . . . He thus found his own way to the new mode of perception which, between 1820 and 1830, became the problem of creation for the most advanced minds in painting—for Constable and Corot, Delacroix and Turner.'

One of Allston's early pupils was Samuel F. B. Morse (1791–1872) who at the age of forty gave up a successful and active career in painting to devote himself to the researches that led to the invention

242

230 WASHINGTON ALLSTON *The Flight of Florimel* 1819

of the telegraph. Taking his cue from Allston, he produced such serene landscapes as *View from Apple Hill* (1828, New York State Historical Society, Cooperstown, N.Y.). As was the case with other American painters of the time, in order to earn a living he was forced into portraiture, in which he combined clarity with strong characterization. Notable for imparting a sense of impetuosity is his over-life-size *Portrait of Lafayette* (1825-6, City Hall, New York), in which the individual is exalted into a symbolic statesman-hero.

Although Allston was no teacher and had little active following, he created an art of mood, of grave and brooding reverie which had a definite filiation down through nineteenth-century American art. In the next generation, the note is struck in the work of John Quidor (1801-81), an eccentric painter of New York about whom very little is known. His subjects were largely inspired by Romantic literature, but with a flavour of uncouth grotesquerie like that of Breughel or Jan Steen. In *Ichabod Crane Pursued by the Headless Horseman* (Yale University Art Gallery), he heightened the eeriness of Washington Irving's tale to an emotional range and power far beyond the source of inspiration. Somewhere between burlesque and terror also is the mood of compositions like *The Devil and Tom Walker* and *Wolfert's Will*. This peculiar style is accomplished by purely painterly means, Quidor's pictures being constructed with a vividly calligraphic brushstroke.

In varying degrees and highly personal directions, the strain of imaginative Romanticism descending from Allston is also found in the work of such individualists as William Page (1811-85) and William Rimmer (1816-79). Page was a controversial figure who divided his time between New York and Rome, painted ideal Romantic allegories like *Cupid and Psyche* (1845) and developed theories of colour to attain maximum resonance of tone. Rimmer— physician, anatomist, sculptor and painter—was capable of producing one of the most hauntingly disturbing visions of the time, *Pursuer and Pursued* (1872, Museum of Fine Arts, Boston).

However, it was not in these esoteric directions that the Romantic dream found its widest expression in America, but rather in representational landscape and picturesque genre. Already in

244

231 THOMAS DOUGHTY (1793–1856) *River Landscape*

Allston's lifetime there grew up what has come to be called the Hudson River School of landscape painting. Impressed by scenic grandeur, both Vanderlyn and Trumbull had painted Niagara Falls. Then came William Dunlap (1766–1839), who painted the Falls in 1815, along with a whole series of views in New York State. But the first artist who can properly be classified as a member of the Hudson River School was Thomas Doughty (1793–1856) who, rather than dealing with scenic wonders, approached landscape with a contemplative and philosophical attitude (*Ill. 231*). Self-taught, he was an ardent hunter and fisherman and his paintings grew out of his love of nature. His first exhibition was in 1824 at the Pennsylvania Academy,

232 ASHER B. DURAND (1796–1886) *Kindred Spirits* 1849

233   THOMAS COLE (1801–48)   *In the Catskills*

234   ASHER B. DURAND   *Imaginary Landscape*

where he showed eight canvases, including two scenes from James Fenimore Cooper's *Pioneers*. Somewhat monotonous in colour and unassuming if not naïve in composition, he was one of the first to see the wild countryside as a theme for painting. Emerson's theories about nature favoured this Romantic inclination, demanding that landscape, renouncing strict Realism, should be illumined and transfigured by the spirit.

In the same mode are the landscapes of Asher B. Durand (1796–1886), who started in New York as an engraver but by 1830 had turned to painting. He studied abroad, and was one of the first Americans to practise painting outdoors. Less poetic than Doughty, his views of the Catskills, of the Mohawk Valley and New England rank him as one of the leading Hudson River School painters (*Ills. 232, 234*). Essentially satisfied with their taste for objective reality, these artists were little concerned with subjecting their views to Classicist ordering or emotional intensification. Yet they rarely sank into a photographic Naturalism lacking in wit and feeling.

The most inventive and articulate member of the Hudson River School was Thomas Cole (1801–48), who was born in England and came to America at an early age. Although he was a fervent admirer of the English Romantic writers, and of Salvator Rosa, whom he appreciated more than Claude because he felt that he was closer to him both aesthetically and humanly ('I believe that I am more at my ease among savagery and torment'), Cole was above all an instinctive artist. His painting is the direct and wholly emotional reflection of the Catskill Mountains (*Ills. 233, 235*). The poet Bryant spoke of 'his primitive and untamed vision', and the description is accurate. A picture like the *Oxbow of the Connecticut* (1836, Metropolitan Museum), with the contrast between the peaceful background and the stormy wind tossing the trees and heaping up the clouds, offers an excellent example of how his art presents immediate and perceptible 'impressions' which grasp nature in a unique way, embracing simultaneously its narrative details and its deep soul.

Cole's Romanticism, which became increasingly close to John Martin's, took on a poignant accent in *Voyage of Life* and *The Cross and the World*: here landscape becomes a cypher language almost

235 THOMAS COLE *Landscape with Tower*

analogous to that of Philipp Otto Runge, where the emotions speak
in the language of allegory. Without distancing himself from reality,
Cole introduced symbolic landscape into the United States. He
adapted it to the primitive and untamed character of the country,
a character very different from that of European nature where
man had tamed the elements, so to speak.

From about 1830 to 1870 the homely manners of rural districts and
picturesque scenes from frontier life made a fertile field for the
painter-observer to record. The prevailing Romanticism became
sublimated in a realism that reflects both the solemn poetry of
unaffected manners and the grandeur of the Western pioneering

249

236 WILLIAM SIDNEY MOUNT (1807–68) *Eel Spearing at Setauket* 1845

experience. In painting, a parallel to Washington Irving's descriptions of country life along the Hudson is the anecdotal painting of William Sidney Mount (1807–68). This singularly natural painter felt no urge to study abroad, no craving for the glories of Italy. In the rural back-water of his native Long Island he produced such compositions as *Eel Spearing at Setauket*, 1845 (*Ill. 236*), in which the glassy water and the farmland in the background are rendered with the clarity of a seventeenth-century Dutch master. Almost completely forgotten until examples of his work recently came to light is Martin Johnson Heade (1814–1904). His views of the Eastern seaboard have an eerie, almost Surrealist quality in the exact rendering of the atmospheric

effects, sometimes—as in *Storm over Narragansett Bay*, 1868 (*Ill. 237*)—
with a sense of impending disaster.

Of the mid-century painters who focused on the Western expansion and frontier life, George Catlin (1796–1872) is almost universally known for bringing the American Indian into fashion. He lived with the Indians, studying and cataloguing with the care and methods of an ethnographer the objects which they used. He collected the results of his researches in a very odd work published in 1841 entitled *Manners, Customs and Conditions of the North American Indians*. Catlin foresaw the disappearance of the Indian and felt it was essential to preserve their images 'before', he said, 'they go to seek their fathers' spirits, towards the setting sun'. Thus he attached more importance to the documentary and informative value of his work than to its artistic quality. Abandoning portraiture, which he had practised with a certain amount of success at the beginning of his career, he left Washington and the majority of his clientele in 1832 and set out for the West, the home of his beloved

237　MARTIN J. HEADE (1814–1904)　*Storm over Narragansett Bay*　1868

238 ALFRED MILLER
(1810–71)
The Trapper's Bride

Red Indians. He returned five years later with a profusion of paintings and drawings; and he also brought back the beginnings of his
Indian Museum—tents, clothes, weapons, utensils, which proved the
accuracy and documentary precision of his paintings.

He was also an excellent illustrator, as was Seth Eastman (1808–
75). Eastman settled in Minnesota in 1830, and lived among the
Sioux and the Chippewas both as friend and portraitist. In this he was
luckier than John Mix Stanley (1814–72), who continually ran the
risk of being murdered by his models. In this connection one should
also mention James Otto Lewis, Charles Bird King, Alfred Miller
(*Ill. 238*) and Karl Bodmer (*Ill. 239*).

An entirely different and startlingly original interpreter of frontier
life was George Caleb Bingham (1811–79), who was born in
Virginia and moved at an early age to Missouri, where he painted a

239 KARL BODMER (1809–93) *Indians Hunting Bison* 1843

series of scenes which he described as 'our social and political consequences'. His famous painting of *Fur Traders Descending the Missouri, c.* 1845 (*Ill. 240*) joins intense and direct veracity with a feeling for nature which transcends the limitations of the subject. In the solitude and mystery of such canvases, Bingham recorded the solemnity and grandeur of remote pioneering experience.

The ultimate development of the Romantic school of landscape painting found its exponent in several painters of Western mountain scenery after mid-century, foremost among whom was Frederick E. Church (1826–1900). Early influenced by Cole, Church soon graduated from the Catskills and moved farther afield. He journeyed to South America, where he painted vast mountain panoramas in Ecuador and Colombia. In Labrador he became fascinated with icebergs, and eventually his travels took him to Italy, Greece, Palestine and Syria.

One must also recognize that the fashion for scenic panoramas, which were all the rage during the first thirty years of the nineteenth century, implied the predominance of the 'landscape of instruction' over the 'landscape of feeling'. Among the most famous producers of panoramas—often recruited among theatrical scene-painters who were sometimes more artisans than artists—one should mention Frederick Catherwood, John Banvard and Henry Lewis, whose works astonish more by their extraordinary dimensions than by their aesthetic value. Lewis' panorama showing the course of the Mississippi on a canvas two-thirds of a mile long, and Banvard's even more gigantic work (five times longer) can only be called artistic curiosities. They are remembered as symptomatic of the American taste for the gigantic and the colossal, the unmeasurable, which in architecture culminated in the skyscraper and in sculpture in the faces of American presidents carved in the side of Mount Rushmore.

The illusionism which appears in the still-lifes of the period appealed to the need for true, objective and absolute realism which is another facet of the American character. John Peto's virtuosity lies in the manner in which he gave a gripping spatial value to objects hung on the wall, following a tradition dear to the eighteenth century. Peto (1854–1907) did not attempt *trompe-l'œil* for its own sake, nor for the puerile pleasure of seeing people holding out their hands to a painted object as if it were real. Whereas the true Romantic painter is always anxious to know and express the individual's position in the universe, in both the moral and physical senses, Peto tried to detach the object from its surroundings and its roots, thus underlining the autonomy of everything and the independence of each element in a still-life, distinct from its neighbours and even in opposition to them.

The case of William Harnett (1848–92) is complex and enigmatic. Born in 1848, he belonged to a much younger generation than did Peto. He seems a tardy Romantic, but in many ways he was more outdated than his predecessor. His paintings remind one of Kalf, Chardin, even Flegel or Baschenis, although he is more lyrical than the latter. Larkin defined the exact nature of Harnett's illusionism: 'When he painted the glowing embers of a pipe one felt their heat,

240 GEORGE CALEB BINGHAM (1811–79) *Fur Traders Descending the Missouri* c. 1845

and when he included a five-dollar bill in his pictures the Treasury Department began to get worried.'

Harnett stands out from landscape painters as a Romantic in his intensification of reality and in his singular power of suggestion emanating from his subtle lampoons and the 'lying mysteries' that they perhaps contain. A composition like *Old Models* (*Ill. 241*) in the Boston Museum is strong and subtly constructed, and its geometrical substructure is almost as rigorous as that of a Mondrian. To be properly understood, it must be placed within the old tradition of the *vanitas* still-life.

255

241 WILLIAM HARNETT (1848–92)
Old Models 1892

Edward Hicks (1780–1849) and Erastus Field, among the American Romantics, are two forerunners of Surrealism who lead us towards the fantastic. Hicks is quite close to the so-called 'naïve-painters', while Field is oddly related to the mysterious Monsû Desiderio, whose paintings he had certainly never seen. It is difficult to imagine a stranger character than Hicks: this Quaker farmer from Pennsylvania, the Douanier Rousseau of the New World, only reluctantly devoted his leisure hours to painting after painful struggles of conscience. Although he was always careful not to paint anything which was outside the bounds of innocence or usefulness, he believed that in this way the profane frivolity of art could be purified. Hicks, who was an itinerant preacher, intended his painting to edify and moralize; that is why he transposed verses from the Bible into his

242   EDWARD HICKS (1780–1849)   *Peaceable Kingdom*

simple and exquisite compositions as readily as he took them as texts
for his sermons.

He was most often inspired by the verse in Isaiah announcing a
future earthly paradise where universal peace will be restored to the
joy and happiness of all creatures. The two best versions of this story of
the *Peaceable Kingdom*, which had such a hold on him, are to be found
in the Brooklyn Museum (*Ill. 242*) and in the Phillips Collection in
Washington. But it is said that there are more than eighty versions,
and in them certain themes are repeated. In a corner of the picture
one usually sees a group of 'palefaces' conversing with some 'Red-
skins' and discussing with them the voluntary cession, subject to
payment, of a part of their territories. In this way America would
become the 'peaceable kingdom' in reality and the quarrels between

the new arrivals and the former masters of the continent would be ended. In this Eden wild animals lie down without posing any danger to the neighbouring cows, deer and sheep. Lions and tigers, who look out proudly from these pictures in an impressive confrontation, can afford to open their eyes widely and frighteningly, for one knows that now they are harmless and that children may freely lie between their paws and climb over their backs.

Erastus Salisbury Field (1805–1900) has neither the enjoyable clumsiness nor the child-like soul of the master of the 'Peaceable Kingdom'; one feels that he was haunted by archaeological cares, by memories of a grandiose and mysterious architecture taken from old books. He was very impressed by the gigantic monuments of Egypt, and also by their connections with the Hebrew people as recounted in the Bible. While painting portraits and landscapes, Field reproduced his architectural visions, touched by the same breath of the Old Testament that touched John Martin and his illustrations for *Paradise Lost*. At the same time he aspired to a colossal syncretism wherein the old and the new are mingled, and which in its best moments is the work of a genuine visionary.

Field's most remarkable creation in this area, which is without equivalent in American and perhaps in European art, is the unlikely *Historical Monument of the American Republic* which he painted towards the end of his life to glorify his country. He employed an immense canvas and began constructing an extraordinary group of towers of Babel joined at their summits by aerial bridges, swarming with sculptures, bas-reliefs and colonnades. He mingles in an extravagant amalgamation the styles of India, Egypt, Greece, Mesopotamia and Rome with the quiet and imperturbable daring of a man who never doubted the reality of his dreams.

The tremendous advance of industry and commerce in the United States, with the pride and feeling of power which were its consequence, created in both the artistic world and in the general public a current of opinion which favoured a type of painting completely freed from the Old World and European models. Henceforth they devoted their attention to what Weir called 'palpable truth', to discovering 'characteristic moments' and only keeping the 'expressive

243 THOMAS EAKINS (1844–1916) *The Biglen Brothers Racing* 1873

values' of contemporary society. Romantic Realism, as in the still-lifes of Harnett and Peto, gave way to striking images which depicted unequivocally the present day.

If we summarize the ambitions of American artists during the period that corresponds to European Realism and Naturalism, we realize that, to borrow words from one of the most brilliant of them, their aim was 'to examine the heart of American life'. These were the words of Thomas Eakins (1844–1916), all of whose work illustrates this desire to break with the traditions of the past. However, the split was not total since a contemporary of Eakins, A. P. Ryder (1847–1917), stayed resolutely Romantic, as is demonstrated by his famous painting of *Siegfried and the Rhine Maidens* (*Ill. 244*). But this painter's

244 ALBERT PINKHAM RYDER (1847–1917) *Siegfried and the Rhine Maidens* c. 1875

position was unusual; he lived apart from others in a wretched studio unknown to art-lovers and collectors, shut into his dreams and isolated from reality, as if he were living in an enchanted world.

Thomas Eakins, on the other hand, was so exclusively Realist (*Ill. 243*) that he often worked from photographs which he himself had taken, fearing that his imagination might alienate him from raw objectivity. Perhaps he remembered the two *Anatomy Lessons* by

Rembrandt when he painted *The Gross Clinic* (Jefferson Medical College, Philadelphia), but this is nothing more than a record of events, no matter how remarkably painted. And although it is one of his best paintings, it is as soulless as a snapshot. Eakins lacked human warmth and sympathy because he was enslaved by the 'slice of life' attitude. But these very qualities are found in Winslow Homer (1836–1910), who combined the functions of artist and illustrator with that of war correspondent (he was with the Army of the Potomac during the Civil War). This reporter had delicate and vivid perceptions together with a warm love for nature; his marine paintings, of which the Washington *Breezing Up* (*Ill. 245*) is an excellent example, are as full of poetry as the Dutch seascapes of the seventeenth century.

245 WINSLOW HOMER (1836–1910) *Breezing Up* 1873

246   EASTMAN JOHNSON (1824–1906)   *Not at Home*

The 'slice of life' which Winslow Homer preferred was that of the
Adirondack woods and the New England coast. Eastman Johnson
found his on the battlefields of the Civil War, in the forests of Maine
and among the sand dunes of Nantucket; but he had first of all learned
to paint from Leutze in Düsseldorf and Thomas Couture in Paris,
and one may place him in the tradition of the European 'Intimists'.
There is a similar analogy between such a painting as *Not at Home*

247 WILLIAM MERRITT CHASE (1849–1916) *A Friendly Call*

(*Ill. 246*) and the 'genre scenes' of the Belgian Henri de Braekeleer, and *A Friendly Call* (*Ill. 247*) by Johnson's compatriot William Merritt Chase (1849–1916).

There is no science or academic formula in the technique of Linton Park (1826–1906). He was a cabinet-maker, just as the Douanier Rousseau was employed in the Customs, and he incarnates the true spirit of American painting in the nineteenth century. He is naïve in his manner of presenting picturesque scenes from daily life and in his vision of beings and objects. His ambition was to reproduce reality in its purest state, but to this he added a fervent candour and a freshness of heart and vision; in the twentieth century these are the virtues of Grandma Moses.

Is it possible to place Mary Cassatt (1845–1926) and James McNeill Whistler (1834–1903) in a purely American school? The former left her native land while still quite young and made her career in France working alongside Degas and Manet, and perhaps also in their wake. It is almost impossible to find a specifically American character in her paintings. As for Whistler, he belongs both in time and in taste to Symbolism. His refinement (rendered more acute by his observation of the Japanese), his considered chromaticism and his compositions where the colours are orchestrated delicately like musical instruments in a symphony: all these place him at the opposite pole from the narrow Naturalistic aesthetic of the Weir brothers, who were apostles of Eakins' creed of 'palpable truth' and 'the heart of American life'. At a time which saw the apogee of Naturalism, Whistler declared himself an enemy of 'that damned realism'. He turned his back on nature, creating another nature for his own use in accordance with his fancy. He travelled in a dream-world different from that of the Romantics, but just as unreal, as systematically invented or, rather, re-invented.

Whistler was a revolutionary in the strongest sense of the word. When the 'Salon des Refusés' first revealed his talent to Paris in 1863 a new era began, with a conception of form and colour which heralded the great upheavals of the last years of the nineteenth century and the first years of the twentieth.

Selected Bibliography

List of Illustrations

Index

Selected Bibliography

For surveys in English of the Romantic movement in those countries not listed below, see the relevant sections in the books given under *General*.

General

BRION, M. *Romantic Art*, London and New York, 1960

KLINGENDER, F. D. *Art and the Industrial Revolution*, London, 1947

NOVOTNY, F. *Painting and Sculpture in Europe 1780–1880*, Harmondsworth and Baltimore, 1960

PEVSNER, N. *Art and Architecture 1830–1870*, Cambridge, 1957

RICHARDSON, E. P. *The Way of Western Art 1776–1914*, Cambridge, Mass., 1939

Architecture

ADDISON, A. E. *Romanticism and the Gothic Revival*, New York, 1938

HAMLIN, T. F. *Greek Revival Architecture in America*, London and New York, 1944

HITCHCOCK, H. R. *Architecture: Nineteenth and Twentieth Centuries*, Harmondsworth, 1958, 2nd edn. Baltimore, 1963

KAUFMANN, E. *Three Revolutionary Architects: Boullée, Ledoux and Lequeu*, Philadelphia, 1952
– *Architecture in the Age of Reason*, Cambridge, Mass., 1955

NEWTON, R. H. *Town and Davis: Architects*, New York, 1942

PEVSNER, N. *An Outline of European Architecture*, 3rd edn. London, 1948 and Baltimore, 1960

Sculpture

BELL, C. F. *Annals of Thomas Banks*, Cambridge, 1938

CONSTABLE, W. G. *John Flaxman*, London, 1927

MOLESWORTH, H. D. *European Sculpture*, London and New York, 1965

Painting
England

BAKER, C. H. C. *Crome*, London, 1921

BLUNT, A. *The Art of William Blake*, London and New York, 1959

BOASE, T. S. R. *The Oxford History of English Art, 1800–1870*, London, 1959

CONSTABLE, W. G. *Richard Wilson*, London, 1953

FINBERG, A. J. *The Life of J. M. W. Turner, R.A.* 2nd edn. London, 1960 and New York, 1961

FRY, R. *Reflections on British Painting*, London, 1934

GAUNT, W. A. *A Concise History of English Painting*, London and New York, 1964

GISSING, A. C. *William Holman Hunt: A Biography*, London, 1936

GRIGSON, G. *Samuel Palmer: The Visionary Years*, London, 1947

LESLIE, C. R. *Memoirs of the Life of John Constable*, ed. A. Shirley. London, 1937 and New York, 1951

OPPÉ, A. P. *Alexander and John Robert Cozens*, London, 1952

RIENAECKER, V. G. R. *John Sell Cotman, 1782–1842*, Leigh-on-Sea, 1953

SHIRLEY, A. *Bonington*, London, 1940

STOKES, H. *Girtin and Bonington*, London, 1922

WATERHOUSE, E. K. *Gainsborough*, London, 1958

WILENSKI, R. H. *English Painting*, London, 1964

France

ADHÉMAR, J. *Honoré Daumier*, London, 1954

BERGER, K. *Géricault and His Works*, Lawrence, Kansas, 1955

BOAS, G. (ed.) *Courbet and the Naturalistic Movement*, Baltimore, 1938

BROWN, M. W. *The Painting of the French Revolution*, New York, 1938

FRIEDLAENDER, W. F. *From David to Delacroix*, Cambridge, Mass., 1952

FRY, R. *Characteristics of French Art*, London, 1932

MACK, G. *Gustave Courbet*, London and New York, 1951

WELLINGTON, H. (ed.) *The Journal of Delacroix: A Selection*, London and New York, 1951

WILDENSTEIN, G. *Ingres*, London, 1954 and 2nd rev. edn. New York, 1956

WILENSKI, R. H. *French Painting*, New York, 1938

Spain

CHABRUN, J. F. *Goya*, London, 1965

DELEVOY, R. L. *Goya*, London, 1955

DU GUÉ TRAPIER, E. *Eugenio Lucas y Padilla*, New York, 1940

MALRAUX, A. *Saturn: An Essay on Goya*, London and New York, 1957

POST, C. R. *History of Spanish Painting*, Cambridge, Mass., 1930

TOMORY, P. A. *Goya*, London, 1960

Switzerland

ANTAL, F. *Fuseli Studies*, New York, 1956

MASON, E. C. (ed.) *The Mind of Henry Fuseli*, London, 1951

Italy

BROWN, A. V. and RANKIN, W. *A Short History of Italian Painting*, London and New York, 1936

MATHER, F. J. *A History of Italian Painting*, 2nd edn. New York, 1939

Russia

ETTLINGER, A. and GLADSTONE, J. M. *Russian Literature, Theatre and Art: A Bibliography of Works in English, Published 1900–1945*, London, 1947

TALBOT RICE, T. *A Concise History of Russian Art*, London and New York, 1963

USA

BARKER, V. *American Painting: History and Interpretation*, London and New York, 1953

BAUR, J. I. H. *Eastman Johnson: An American Genre Painter*, New York, 1940

CAHILL, H. and BARR, A. H. JR. (ed.) *Art in America*, New York, 1939

CHRIST-JANER, A. W. *George Caleb Bingham of Missouri*, New York, 1940

COWDREY, B. and WILLIAMS, H. *William Sidney Mount, An American Painter*, New York, 1944

FORD, A. *Edward Hicks: Painter of the Peaceable Kingdom*, Philadelphia, 1952

GOODRICH, L. *Thomas Eakins: His Life and Work*, New York, 1933
– *Winslow Homer*, New York, 1944
– *Albert Pinkham Ryder*, New York, 1947

MARCEAU, H. and KIMBALL, F. *Benjamin West*, Philadelphia, 1938

MCCAUSLAND, E. *George Inness, An American Landscape Painter*, New York, 1946

MCINTYRE, R. *Martin Johnson Heade*, New York, 1948

RICHARDSON, E. P. *Washington Allston: A Study of the Romantic Artist in America*, New York, 1948
– *Painting in America*, New York, 1956

ROSS, M. *The West of Alfred Jacob Miller*, Norman, Okla., 1951

SEAVER, E. *Thomas Cole*, Hartford, Conn., 1949

SWEET, F. *The Hudson River School and the Early American Landscape Tradition*, Chicago, 1945

List of Illustrations

The author and the publishers are grateful to the many official bodies, individuals and institutions mentioned here for their assistance in supplying original illustration material. Measurements are given in centimetres. Height precedes width.

269

273

275

278

Index

Numbers in italic refer to illustrations

Shelley, Percy Bysshe, 78, 240
Stifter, Adalbert, 117
Sigalon, 151
Simon, Friedrich Rudolf, 190
Skovgaard, Peter Kristian, 209
Smargiassi, Gabriele, 213
Sonne, Jorge Valentin, 201-2
Sorolla y Bastida, Joaquín, 189
Speckter, Erwin, 118
Spenser, Edmund, 241
Sperl, Johann, 131
Spitzweg, Karl, *97*, 109, 124, 134, 222
Staël, Madame de, 37, 139
Stanley, John Mix, 252
Steen, Jan, 244
Steinle, Eduard Jacob, 104
Stevens, Alfred, *213*, 224
Stothard, Thomas, *57*, 71
Stubbs, George, *46, 47, 50*, 56-8
Swedenborg, Emmanuel, 50

Tchernichevsky, 230-1
Thoma, Hans, *110, 111*, 11, 122, 124
Tiepolo, Giovanni Battista, 7, 148, 183, 188
Toepffer, Wolfgang Adam, *180*, 190-1
Tolstoy, Leo, 232
Town, Ishiel, 29-30, 31
Trübner, Wilhelm, *119*, 131, 164
Trumbull, Jonathan, *228*, 240, 245
Turner, J. M. W., *62, 63, 64, 65, 66, 67, 68*, 62, 74-8, 88, 160, 240, 242

Uhde, Fritz von, 10, 132, 133, 134, 221

Vanderlyn, John, 240, 245
Van Gogh, Vincent, 156-8, 221
Varley, John, 84
Venetsianov, Alexis, 228
Verdi, Giuseppe, 213
Vereshchagin, Vassily, *222*, 233-4
Vierge, Daniel Urralieta, 189
Viollet-le-Duc, Eugène Emmanuel, *17, 19, 27*

Wächter, Eberhard, 193
Wackenroder, Wilhelm Heinrich, 21, 211
Wagner, Richard, 10, 14, 204
Waldmuller, Ferdinand Georg, 117
Walpole, Horace, *1, 11*, 19, 60
Wappers, Gustave, 216
Ward, James, *48*, 56, 58-9, 70-1
Watteau, Antoine, 7, 134, 155
Watts, George Frederick, 88, 90
Wedgwood, Josiah, 9, 18
Welti, Albert, 123
West, Benjamin, *226*, 55, 238-9, 240
Whistler, James McNeill, 93, 263, 264
Wickenberg, Per Gabriel, 209
Wiertz, Antoine Joseph, *209*, 216, 217-20
Wilson, Richard, *51, 52*, 60-2, 64
Winckelmann, Johann Joachim, 8
Wootton, John, 56
Wright, Joseph, *44*, 55
Wyatt, James, 7, *8*
Wyattville, Sir Jeffrey, *8*, 23

Zola, Emile, 10, 171

286

PRAEGER WORLD OF ART SERIES

ART OF CHINA,
KOREA, AND JAPAN
Peter Swann

ART OF THE
BYZANTINE ERA
David Talbot Rice

THE ART OF
THE RENAISSANCE
Peter and Linda Murray

A CONCISE HISTORY
OF MODERN PAINTING
Sir Herbert Read

THE ART OF
THE ANCIENT NEAR EAST
Seton Lloyd

A CONCISE HISTORY
OF PAINTING
From Giotto to Cézanne
Michael Levey

BAROQUE AND ROCOCO ART
Germain Bazin

EARLY MEDIEVAL ART
John Beckwith

ISLAMIC ART
David Talbot Rice

A CONCISE HISTORY
OF ENGLISH PAINTING
William Gaunt

ROMAN ART
AND ARCHITECTURE
Sir Mortimer Wheeler

GREEK ART
John Boardman

EUROPEAN SCULPTURE
From Romanesque to
Neoclassic
H. D. Molesworth

A CONCISE HISTORY
OF MODERN SCULPTURE
Sir Herbert Read

ANCIENT ARTS OF
CENTRAL ASIA
Tamara Talbot Rice

ANCIENT ARTS OF
THE AMERICAS
G. H. S. Bushnell

A CONCISE HISTORY
OF RUSSIAN ART
Tamara Talbot Rice

PRAEGER WORLD OF ART PROFILES

PICASSO
Pierre Daix

KLEE
Gualtieri di San Lazzaro

CHAGALL
Jean Cassou

SEURAT
John Russell